John Wade Thirlwall

Songs and Poems

John Wade Thirlwall

Songs and Poems

ISBN/EAN: 9783744775700

Printed in Europe, USA, Canada, Australia, Japan

Cover: Foto ©Thomas Meinert / pixelio.de

More available books at **www.hansebooks.com**

SONGS AND POEMS,

BY

JOHN WADE THIRLWALL.

———•———

LONDON:

PUBLISHED BY SAMUEL FRENCH, 89, STRAND.

(Successor to T. H. Lacy.)

———

1872.

Preface.

———◆———

The greater number of the following poems were written
and published singly, many years ago, but I have thought
it unnecessary to place them in chronological order.   I
have nothing to say, as to their merits or demerits ; if
they do not defend themselves, they are not worth de-
fending.   To my subscribers, whose spontaneous assist-
ance has enabled me to produce this volume, I return my
sincere thanks,

And remain,

Their most obedient servant,

JOHN WADE THIRLWALL.

SONGS AND POEMS.

THE DELL-BORN STREAM.

Within a wood-embosom'd dell,
   There gush'd a clear and sparkling spring ;
My playmates called it " fairy well,"
   'Twas bright as sunbeam on the wing :
The waters rose and hurried on,
   Some unseen power forbade their stay ;
They gladden'd all they look'd upon,
   Look'd joyous too, but rush'd away.
Why restless from their very birth ?
They'd find no happier home on earth.

The waters flow'd, and 'twas in vain
   To argue, or forbid their course ;
Each dam we built, them to restrain,
   They bore down with resistless force ;
And through the dell they singing went,
   Where wild flowers and green sedges grew ;
On some great purpose they were bent,
   But what, perchance, they little knew.
If so, they still seem'd to rejoice,
And to the dell gave pleasant voice

A shining stream the spring is soon
  Its banks by bending osiers lined ;
The waters murmur happy tune,
  The willows, harp-strings to the wind :
By cottage lowly now it goes,
  Most welcome to the peasant born ;
Its drink, the only wine he knows,
  That simple taste let no man scorn :
Full many need not now repine,
Had they but known no other wine !

Now troubled is that stream full sore,
  Mid rocky hills its course doth lie ;
The rugged rifts now struggling o'er,
  Now tumbling o'er the chasm high.
The thunder rolls, the lightnings flash,
  The rain pours down, and from each height
The torrent roars with angry dash—
  Where is that stream so glad and bright ?
The drumly waves hold on apace,
The dell-born stream, ah, who can trace ?

'Though alter'd, still it doth not cease,
  But wanders on to find a home ;
Earth will not give the waters peace,
  Absorb'd or fed they still must roam :
It gains the open sea at last,
  And trackless then to human eye,

All record of its fate is past,
  'Tis gone, and yet it cannot die.
Within that open, solemn sea,
The dell-born stream must somewhere be.

Oh ! life is like that pleasant spring,
  No human force its flight can stay ;
For ever, borne on rapid wing,
  And who can tell to whence away ?
The flowers that on its pathway grow,
  Are only for a moment known ;
The brightest moments it can know,
  Are almost ere they're counted, flown.
Eternity, the awful sea,
Where life seems o'er, though still it be !

THOU HOME OF MY CHILDHOOD.

Thou home of my childhood, for long years forsaken,
  So dearly remembered, I come unto thee,
With joy and with reverence, yet bitter thoughts waken,
  A home thou'rt no longer to mine and to me :
The Green, sprinkt with kingcup and daisies before me,
  Where Summer first wooed my frail footsteps to stray ;
But where are the arms, o'er each hollow that bore me,
  The loved and the loving ?   All faded away !

Our garden's unchanged ; and the rose-tree is blooming
   I planted with pride and with glee when a boy ;
Then far away roaming, the sky bright or glooming,
   My mother would tend it, her sorrow, her joy :
You rudely form'd stile, fringed by ash and by willow,
   Was framed by Auld Johnny, short time ere he died ;
I knew not of death, and when borne from his pillow,
   I marvell'd—and thought he turned towards me and
      sighed.

How little is changed ; all around the same flowers,
   The oak and the elm spread their arms as of yore ;
The blue sea is rolling by Warkworth's grey towers,
   And white billows flash, as they break on the shore ;
And oh ! how sublime is the roar of that ocean,
   'Tis wonderful still, 1 can list as a child ;
And so it will be, when life's wilder emotion,
   Is stilled, and my steps can no more be beguiled.

I gaze on our cot, till my heart's half believing
   The walls teem with gladness and welcome me here ;
Thou home of my childhood, my heart's to thee cleav-
      ing,
   The days of lang syne, ah, must ever be dear :
To strangers thou'rt given, my kindred departed,
   Like leaves in the keen blast of Autumn they fell ;
And I, old and feeble, and half broken hearted,
   Have come, ere I die, but to bid you farewell !

SONG OF THE FATES.

Seasons come, seasons go,
  Rest we not, night or day ;
Rest alone, can we know
  When all time's past away ;
For the Fates never sleep
  And the Fates never slept,
They have seen the world weep,
  The Fates never wept !
Spin the thread, sisters mine,
Coarse and strong, frail and fine.

Mark, this frail thread is new,
  'Tis a life just begun ;
Joy from nations is due,
  'Tis a monarch's one son ;
Their rejoicings are deep—
  But this fibre is thin,
The nations must weep,
  Cut the thread, 'twill not spin.
Twist and twine, twist and twine,
Coarse and strong, frail and fine.

Here's a starved miser's thread,
  Weak is he, weak and old,
Heart he has, all but dead,
  Panting only for gold :

Love and friendship unknown,
  Hoarding on through long years ;
For himself lived alone,
  Dead to smiles, dead to tears.
Cut the thread ! sister mine,
Coarse or strong, frail or fine.

See, these threads fondly blend,
  Spin them well, spin them true ;
There, two fond hearts depend,
  Hopes so bright, joys so new.
And their hopes—must they fade ?
  And their joys—must they die ?
'Twas to mourn they were made,
  We our task but to ply !
Twist and twine, twist and twine,
Coarse and strong, frail and fine.

THE SHADOW ON THE BLIND.

The sky all darkness, the unquiet wind
  Now fitful darting from its airy bed,
Bounds like a deer when hunters are behind,
  Now pillows on some grassy knoll its head :
It is not storm, a calm appears still less,
  Nor war nor peace ; but like a lover's heart
When love and jealousy together press,
  The one to heal, the other rend apart ;

And One, amid the darkness and the wind,
Stays, watching yonder Shadow on the Blind.

The light within doth taunt the sullen night ;
    What comfort, what content that window beams ;
The Shadow, now gigantic, and now slight,
    Now dreamy, now an angel-outline seems :
And underneath that dark funereal pine
    Whose nodding, hearse-like plumes so rise and fall,
The youth remains ; does hope within him shine,
    Or hopeless love his drooping heart enthrall ?
What sympathy, what comfort can he find,
In watching yonder Shadow on the Blind.

The gusty breeze doth fold its wings in peace,
    A voice melodious charms Night's listening ear ;
No wonder all discordant things should cease,
    'Tis from yon window I the music hear :
The casement opens, and a gentle face
    Looks through the darkness up into the sky
As if her glance could reach the throne of grace
    The angels, the immortal-blest descry.
The youth doth kneel—go, shield thee from the wind,
The light is gone, no Shadow on the Blind.

THE LAST OWL OF KIRKSTALL

The moonlight grey on Kirkstall fell,
    All at the midnight hour,
The wild wind shook the rusted bell,
    High in the crumbling tower ;
" Hoo, hoo," the lonely owlet cried,
    From a tomb defaced and old ;
" Hoo, hoo," the vaults of death replied,
    And the wind that whistled cold.
And hark ! with solemn dreary sound,
    From yonder cloisters wide,
A choral chaunt doth swell around,
    And hooded spectres glide.
Still by that ancient, nameless tomb,
    The owl hoots on amid the gloom.

  .   .   .   .

Says Frederique, " my weapon true
    Shall tame that creature's pride ;
And be it ghost or bird, I vow,
    It shall not there abide,"
Flash went the steel, the bullet sped,
    The shrieking owl upsprang ;
The walls of Kirkstall shook with dread,
    Sepulchral echoes rang.

  .   .   .   .

Leoda's bell afar doth toll
    The midnight hour in vain ;

It brings not back the lonely owl,
 And shadowy spectre train ;
The wind alone through Kirkstall walls,
 Is heard at dead of night ;
Save when some carven fragment falls,
 Time trod on in his flight.

 . . . .

But why is Frederique so pale,
 Why gleam his eyes so wild ?
His infant's laugh to charm doth fail,
 He smiles not on his child :
All human hopes, all human fears,
 Have ceased to touch his heart ;
To win him back to smiles or tears
 Surpasseth mortal art.

And oft he seeks the abbey gloom
 And fainly would he find,
The owl upon its ancient tomb
 Wail to the wailing wind.
But what him ails, or what his woe,
Man knows not, and can never know !

THE HOUND AND THE HORN.

Arouse brother sportsmen, to horse, and again
Sweep on like a whirlwind o'er mountain and plain ;
The grain it is garner'd the sky bright and clear,
So hurrah ! for the chase and the fleet-footed deer.

Amid fashion and pomp how I long'd for the morn,
That should bring the glad music of hound and of horn;
With the bold merry hearts of the old English breed,
Ever ready to fight for their country and creed.
Trala la, trala la, come awaken the morn
With the soul-thrilling music of hound and of horn.

The breeze freshly blows and the dew glistens bright,
The hounds bay impatient, the lark 'gins his flight;
The mist steals away from the green-breasted vale,
Tis a morn of all others true hearts love to hail.
Thus my fathers of old called your sires from their rest
Whether battle or chase, it was joy to their breast;
And those time-honour'd walls oft have rung to the cheer,
When they met for the fight, or the chase of the deer.
Trala la, trala la, come awaken the morn
To the soul thrilling music of hound and of horn.

The time will arrive too, when we must give place,
And those plains cease to ring with our glad horn of chase;
And the knight and the squire and the yeoman so tall,
Be deaf to the horn, unaroused by the call;
So be it, we've revell'd in sunshine so bright,
When day's on the wane, never shrink from the night;
The sons that we cherish will keep up the game,
Their forefathers honour, and rival in fame.
Trala la, trala la, come awaken the morn
With the soul-thrilling music of hound and of horn.

CHRISTMAS.

Come in, Old Christmas, through the changeful year,
No visitor more welcome, or more dear ;
Like an old cloak, we cast away our care
To welcome thee, a blessing everywhere ;
"T'would be a sin to harbour one regret
When thou appearest, none should sigh or fret.

We see the grey, grey beard, the reverend head,
The wrinkled temples, with scant locks bespread,
The smile so bland, good nature in each line,
Religion, peace and love, in love combine ;
We bow to thee, not as a monarch crowned—
By fond affection, loving duty bound.

When first we saw thee, in our early day,
Thou wert as now, gave hearts their kindest play,
In thee is mingled sage and hopeful boy,
The brow of Wisdom, brightened o'er with with joy.
When age is genial, kind, and memory green,
No source of greater happiness hath been.

The spring gives promise, growing summer warms,
And autumn ripens, through rude blasts alarms ;
But thou art perfect, storm or calm the same,
We know thy worth ! in naught art thou to blame ;
Or blinding sleet, or snow, or biting blast,
Come in, Old Christmas, all our hearts thou hast.

Time's mirror, memory, is ever by,
We cannot veil it, howsoe'er we try,
And in it stealthily will ever peep
Past years, and o'er its truthful surface sweep.
Their well remembered features make us glad,
Although the light of joy gives shadows sad ;
We see old friends, the friends we loved the best,
Friends who have done their work, and gone to rest,
Our labours are not closed, life's duties still
Our energies require, our heart, and will ;
We may not throw our sword and shield aside,
Because some brother on the field hath died.

While Heaven doth grant us time, we still must fight
For life, for honour, recognition, right ;
Unto ourselves, at least, we should be true,
Altho' the hounds, in full cry, meet our view.
It would be strange, but that 'tis always so,
Man's chiefest joy, hath still a tinge of woe ;
I Christmas meet, with heart full well inclined,
The bow of care and sorrow to unbind ;
I ope the shining coffers of my joy,
Out glide pale phantoms that would all destroy.
Begone reflection ! welcome Christmas dear ;
To all the world, a blessing, and good cheer.

WHO GOES THERE?

Amid the darkness of the night,
 When foes entrenched before him lie ;
The Sentinel must hold him well,
 And DARE to live, nor FEAR to die.
Each leaf moved by the wind doth sound
 Like footfall of a stealthy foe,
Who through the curtains dark of night
 His arm would stretch to strike the blow ;
So wary Sentinel prepare,
And night affright with " Who goes there ?"

The weary march he has endured,
 The toil upon the battle field,
Full well have tuned him for repose,
 But sleep avaunt, he must not yield ;
Should once he slumber on his post,
 Detected then by friend or foe,
Short time for shrift, for mercy none,
 The ready bullet lays him low !
So wary Sentinel prepare,
And night affright with " Who goes there ?"

Thus balanced between life and death,
 Alive to danger, fearing none,
The manly heart amid its cares,
 With sweetest tenderness beats on :

And fancy on the rayless sky,
   His cottage home doth fondly trace,
He hears the music of each voice,
   Dwells lovingly on each dear face.
Still doth the Sentinel prepare
And night affright with " Who goes there ?"

Brave soldier, thus confronting fate,
   No moment sure, he never quails,
So long as he has limb and breath,
   Our brave defender never fails:
His country's honour still he guards,
   Counts odds as nought, braves every foe;
The British soldier should have friends
   In all that British freedom know ;
When age and suffering show the wear,
None should be blind to " Who goes there ? "

THE AULD WIFE.

The auld wife sits by the fire,
   When winter nights are lang,
And aye, as she turns her wheel,
   She croons some auld Scotch sang.
The wheel, with a birr and a hum,
   Gaes round as she plies her rock ;
The grey cat purrs by the fire,
   And tick tac goes the clock.

The auld wife ance was young,
　　As each auld wife has been ;
But mickle of joy and sorrow
　　Cam youth and age between ;
Now she talks and she sings of old times,
　　When naebody's bye to hear,
And sometimes the auld body laughs,
　　And sometimes she drops a tear.

She thinks of the blythesome time,
　　When young herds cam to woo ;
" Alack !" cries the silly wife,
　　" Wha'd think to see me noo ?"
She thinks of the merry bells
　　That rang when at kirk she wed ;
And then of the mouldy stane
　　That haps the guid man's head.

" My puir old man is gane,
　　His bairns have ceased to weep,
And sae 'twill be with me
　　When I sleep the kirk-yard sleep ;
Bells for bridals will ring,
　　The auld gie place to the young,
Summer will come and go,
　　And auld wives' sangs be sung."

Yet still does she sit by the fire
　　When winter nights are lang,

And aye as she turns her wheel,
   She croons some auld Scotch sang ;
And she talks and she sings of auld times,
   When naebody's bye to hear,
And sometimes the auld body laughs,
   And sometimes she drops a tear.

ALLY MALONE.

Night comes in tears, cold gusts are sweeping,
   O'er the wide waters and mist-shrouded plain ;
Weep murky skies, weep with my weeping,
   Wail on ye cold winds, and join my sad strain :
Soon shall my voice and my wild harp be silent,
   A l that gave life to their music has flown ;
I loved thee dearly, truly, sincerely,
   But thou hast left me, sweet Ally Malone.

Loud blows the wind, but in its closes
   Mirth's joyous shout from yon cabin doth swell ;
Friends in whose bosoms, bright honour reposes,
   Long may you happy be, true hearts farewell :
Once in your sports and your mirth I was foremost,
   Now I am hopeless, complaining alone ;
Joy all forsaking, this fond heart breaking,
   All for thy sake, faithless Ally Malone.

Green Isle farewell, mountain and valley,
  Winds and wild waters soon bear me away
On thy loved shores, no longer 1 dally,
  Bright hope hath flown, despair hath its prey ;
Mid darkness and storm, on the shelterless desert,
  My heart, with love throbbing, is ruthlessly thrown ;
But now we are parting and parting for ever,
  Be thine my last blessing, false Ally Malone.

SUSPENSE; A SKETCH FROM LIFE.

Will the Postman never come ?
I've listened anxiously since morn,
Sometimes with hope, but oft forlorn,
His quick rat-tat to hear :
The hour-glass never seemed so slow,
The sluggish sand forgets to flow ;
The clock—I watch its silent face,
Each quarter seems an hour to trace—
Will the postman never come ?

Your answer shall 1 never have—
Dear Ellen, wilt thou be my wife ?
On that depends my joy, my life !
Shall I be wretched, or most blest ?
Will she be mine I love the best ?

The postman soon my fate reveals,
Tho' he no woe or transport feels ;
No answer, and I'm answered no,
And I must every hope forego—
Will the Postman never come ?

I hear his rat-tat now afar,
It comes like distant sound of war,
Be still my heart—does fortune lour ?
Oh, dread suspense, distracting hour :
He knocks ! no, 'tis my neighbour's door,
Now blest am I, or hope no more ;
He comes, and o'er his precious stock
He casts his eye—and will not knock !
The cruel postman hurries on,
And with him all my hopes are gone.

THE TWO LAMPS.

Give me the lamp ! I would explore,
The silent region of the past ;
And ere my graveward march is o'er
A glance where I have trodden, cast.

.   .   .   .   .   .

It seems a desert bare I trace,
All but in vain my footprints seek,
Tho' here and there, a peopled place,
The lamp of memory's dull and weak.

I gaze, years flit oblivious by,
Friends rise, their history half forgot,
Now misty groups arrest the eye,
Where known, how named, recorded not.
Each day, forgotten as it flows,
Each joy forgotten when 'tis gone,
But conscience, keener, stronger grows
And ever at the heart beats on.

Give me the lamp ! I would explore,
The Future, and Hope's lamp is bright ;
It lights me to a happy shore,
Where discord ends, friends reunite,
Then trim the boat with honest care,
Adown the stream of life to glide,
Let truth unsullied steer us fair,
We heed not storms with such a guide.

THE HARP OF ISABELLE.

Who wakes the Harp of Isabelle,
Now that Isabelle is dead,
And flowers are springing o'er her head ?
It is her lover, sad and pale,
Whose numbers to the midnight wail,
His quenchless love, undying grief,
Thus find in living sound relief.

Ah ! who would rest with Isabelle,
Now that Isabelle is dead,
And flowers are springing o'er her head?
It is her lover there would lie,
Should fate him call, he'd gladly die ;
More dear to him her ashes cold,
Than life and fame, than crowns and gold.

He wakes the Harp of Isabelle,
The lays she loved are on the air,
Angelic murmurs tremble round,
The voice of Isabelle seems there !
" Revisit not this cold dull earth,
Return unto thy world so bright ;
Whilst I remain, the thought of thee,
Will make e'en sorrow, full of light."

THE COTTAGE GARDEN.

In a garden rich in roses,
Freshest green, and fragrant posies,
Stood the dwelling of a maiden,
Walls of white, some ivy-laden ;
Oft her bloomy treasure tending,
I've beheld her graceful wending,
She, the garden most adorning,
Fresh and fair as summer morning.

In that garden, weeds and grasses,
Bend and moan each wind that passes;
Roofless is that humble dwelling,
Desolation round it swelling ;
Gone, the graceful footstep bounding,
Gone, the voice, angelic sounding.

Seek her not by wood or river,
Ask of time, or the time-giver,
Where the maid with beauty glowing,
Where the sunny ringlets flowing ;
Little record earth retaineth,
What it loseth, what it gaineth ;
Peaceful is poor Ellen's haven,
On a stone her name is graven !

THE SWALLOW-NEST.

Within a garden, rich in fruit and flower,
   Attractive to the bee, and bird of song,
Our cottage stood ; a home within a bower ;
   By hawthorn fenced, bloom-laden, thick and strong ;
And here and there the graceful ash upsprang,
   Of various growth and ever varied line ;
And roses o'er the pendant boughs would hang,
   Tall hollyhocks their rainbow tints combine.
Blue in the east, roll'd on the living sea,
Now roaring wild, now murmuring tranquilly.

Above my window once a swallow came,
　　With patient labour fashioned forth a nest;
I marvelled such weak architect could frame,
　　A home so perfect for her weary breast:
My prying gaze at first her fear awoke,
　　That vanished soon, and I might watch at will;
Methinks she read the thoughts that o'er me broke,
　　Believed the boy would guard and never kill;
Within that nest she rear'd her young with care,
And oft the captur'd fly to them would bear.

Thus went the summer with its flowers and light,
　　Thus went the summer seeming but a day;
Time is most fleet when hearts and homes are bright,
　　When heavy grief comes on, he seems to stay.
As autumn laden with ripe fruit appear'd,
　　My winged friend had more familiar grown,
Would by me sweep when at its home I peer'd,
　　Or wieding through the fields and lanes alone;
But rude and keen came winter's herald blast,
And o'er the scene blank desolation cast

The forest shiver'd, leaves like raindrops fell,
　　Thro' naked branches shrieked the cruel wind;
The swallows, heaven directed, knew full well,
　　A far off sunny clime they now must find:

From every quarter came they numbers vast,
    Excited twittering, greeted as they met,
And when my swallow swept the window past,
    The last time, ah ! I never can forget ;
On, on they sail'd upon the wild wind free,
Out o'er the open sky, the open sea.

A star had fallen from my little sky,
    A tear had dimm'd where joy was bright before ;
The lonely nest deserted caught mine eye,
    I never thought to see its tenant more :
Bleak winter past ; when spring rose from her sleep,
    With buds profuse, sweet airs, and grasses new,
As morning flung her blushes o'er the deep,
    I heard a sound—the bird ! could it be true ?
I ope'd the window ; twittering there with glee
The happy swallow, back to home and me.

THE RAIN.

The midnight darkness shrouds the dismal sky,
No rays of light through clouds a loophole find,
Bright flashes only light the lonely scene,
Revealed, then swallowed by the dark profound ;
The hack, the carriage, hurriedly sweep by,
Home, or a shelter, thought of every mind,
The dreadful thunder, silence deep between,
The heavy rain-drops from the pavement bound.

Poor ragged starvelings huddle there,
To shield them from the ruthless storm,
Forgetting all their heavier care,
Tho' hungry, houseless is each form :
To add to such a load of woe,
Seems needless, cruel ; deeper still,
However deep, may misery go,
And darts more keen, than those that kill.

And can it be ? that gilded car,
Those trappings bright of rank and power ;
Can even they not tempests bar,
Must they endure this fearful hour ?
The lightning, thunder, floods of rain,
Alike on prince and outcast fall ;
For all earth's kings will not refrain,
There is One Kingdom over all.

The earth was thirsty, and the food of man,
And bird and beast was withering in the sun ;
The herald of a famine that had swept
From earth the things that graze, and those that creep
The fowls that roost, the birds that cleave the air,
The flowers that make earth lovely, all had died,
The roots and fruits, the green refreshing grass,
Must all have perished, from the land cut off.
But God in mercy sends this plenteous rain,
To plump the wasting grain, make grasses grow,
And Nature's granary with abundance store.

For such a blessing all should thanks return,
Although a dripping cloak or skin they mourn.

THE BIRTH-DAY CLUB.

In Birmingham choice spirits meet,
　　Beneath a goodly roof ;
And nightly they each other greet,
　　From meaner souls aloof :
By friendship and affection bound,
　　They seek no higher range ;
A happier band was never found,
　　They cannot wish to change.
For want of better name, they dub
Their brotherhood, the Birth-day Club.

Each member, on his natal day,
　　A baron of beef must give ;
And furnish else, whate'er he may,
　　The rule, whilst he doth live.
The baron's bone is painted then,
　　As black as nigger's face ;
And hung up in the gaze of men
　　The court-yard walls to grace.
And happy he, allowed to dub
Himself, one of the Birth-day Club.

Full many baron's bones are hung
    Upon those dreary walls ;
And time has many changes rung,
    For he most varied falls :
Some brethren can their baron's count
    From youth, to decent age ;
The fate of some could not surmount
    The first bone on life's page.
They lived a year, their names to dub
As brethren of the Birth-day Club.

On winter nights the cruel blast,
    With rattle and with creak ;
Pours through these honour'd relics fast,
    And now they moan and shriek :
And shadowy forms are seen to ride
    Upon the angry wind ;
These relics sweeping o'er with pride,
    Or greeting them most kind.
'Tis said, and who the thought would snub,
They once were Members of the Club.

'Tis true, each year some one departs,
    Another takes his place ;
The missing, dear to many hearts,
    None new can quite efface :

But still the circle is the same,
  There is no empty chair;
Some one's accepted, who can blame,
  He may be less—more rare.
He gives his baron, and doth dub
Himself one of the Birth-day Club.

I chanced to see those dreary bones,
  And asked why there they hung;
Their history, told in jocund tones,
  I seriously have sung:
The milestones of man's joy and woe,
  As those dark baron's seem'd;
Made thoughts of other days to flow,
  Now storms, now sunshine beam'd.
And now 'twas triumph, now 'twas snub,
With all, as with the Birth-day Club.

Whate'er our circle, we have found
  Some diamonds drop away;
But still, as human we are bound
  To gems of living ray:
We may not like them quite as well,
  But can't bring back the dead;
Whate'er regrets our bosoms swell,
  Restores not blossoms shed.
Long life and happiness to those that dub
Them brethren of the Birth-day Club.

MUSIC ON THE WATER.

On the calm river at the midnight hour,
   We spread our sail, but slumbering was the wind ;
It scarce had stolen perfume from the flower,
   And so our boat was to the tide resigned :
It glided on, the river seem'd asleep,
   And in its dreams a gentle murmur gave,
The moonbeams faintly through a haze would peep,
   The water scatter'd pearls in each faint wave ;
Not pearls alone, but gems of every hue,
More rich and strange than any earth e'er knew.

Time takes our memories as it takes our years,
   I hold slight recollection of our crew ;
But there was one, fond memory still reveres,
   I know not why, time passed her as he flew ;
I think I hear her now, awake the song
   In that calm night upon the dreamy tide,
Now low and sweet, empassioned now and strong,
   Her fingers tinkling the guitar beside :
A living soul seemed born in every tone,
'Twas worth a life those moments to have known.

Her dark eyes now were veil'd, now flashing light,
   And when she ceased to sing, the heart was still,
As when we gaze on sunset splendour bright,
   Then find clouds gather, evening dark and chill

My heart was full, but chastened, so my praise
    Partook of both, she listened with a smile,
Discoursed so sweetly, with such winning ways,
    Her artless magic might a saint beguile ;
How strange that memory should have lost the rest,
Yet graven that bright form upon my breast.

Our sleepy voyage seem'd to me most fleet,
    Impatient spirits blamed the wind and river ;
If fate had made it endless deeming meet,
    I should have kissed the rod, and blessed the giver.
The boat achieved the shore too soon for me,
    From dream of bliss 'tis hard to be awoke ;
No more shall I such happy voyage see,
    No more receive the joy that o'er me broke.
How strange it is, that after many years,
That night returns with smiles, almost with tears.

EVER COMING, EVER GOING.

Throughout a beauteous summer day,
Youth rambled amid nature's sweets,
Admiring oft, and now in play,
What beauty, and what charm he meets ;
With agile limb and spirit high,
He threaded wilds and clomb the hill,
And all was lovely to his eye,
Or mountain stream, or valley rill.

But Time's a river ever flowing,
Ever coming, ever going.

Poor child, he only knew the spring,
With bud and blossom in its lap,
He beauty saw and not its wing,
His heart knew not of Care the tap ;
The sky was bright and beautiful,
His heart beat light with health and joy,
He saw some wights, careworn and dull,
And wondered, being but a boy.
He knew not time was ever flowing,
Ever coming, ever going.

At length, when day was nearly done,
He rested by a river strong ;
Fatigued, the flowery wealth late won,
He threw, the wave bore it along ;
Fleet glided one by one away
The blue-bell, violet and rose ;
In vain regret they cannot stay,
" And are life's blossoms borne like those ? "
He half imagined time was flowing,
Ever coming, ever going.

The sunset glory roused anew
His energy and wonder great,
And up he sprang, and ran or flew
Up to the hill with joy elate ;

What palaces, what hills of gold,
What heavenly splendour greets his sight,
But ere the treasure he had told,
It faded into gloomy night.
He found that Time was ever flowing,
Ever coming, ever going.

RAVENSPURN.*

Mid clouds of varied hue,
Red, orange, purple, grey, and green and gold,
The sun went down, and moaning winds blew cold,
And on my mantle heavy fell the dew ;
The breakers on the shore
Now sullen roar'd, now came with angry sweep
Blue mists afar, moved slowly o'er the deep,
The white sea gull had ceas'd to scream and soar.
Thus gazing all alone,
A figure from the tumbling breakers strode,
In raiment quaint and dark, that lustrous glowed,
And mournful, rested on a weedy stone.
My wonder banish'd fear ;
Out o'er the pathless cliff away I found,
Despite the loosen'd stones that threatening bound ;
The vision spake, and I was by to hear :—

* A port on the coast of Holderness, washed away by the
sea long ago. Its site is now from two to three miles from
the shore.

" The sea rolls over Ravenspurn,
O'er all I loved, o'er all I mourn ;
Five hundred years have passed away,
And yet my fault is green to-day.
And ages rise and fall like waves,
Great men spring up to fill their graves ;
And yet my fault I still must mourn,
Tho' seas roll over Ravenspurn.

My love was beauteous as the day,
She trusted, how could I betray ;
Unworthy I to fill a grave,
Far too unworthy grace to crave :
She was an angel, o'er her light
I spread a darkness and a blight ;
My fault I evermore must mourn,
Tho' seas roll over Ravenspurn.

The greenwood where I vowed to love ;
That vow so register'd above,
I now must seek within the sea,
Alack, that e'er she trusted me.
The ocean hides our meeting place,
But never can her wrongs efface ;
The ages die, I still must mourn,
And seek her grave in Ravenspurn."

With solemn step, and slow,
The mourner o'er the wild waves went,
To seek his love, so injured bent,
Deep in the ocean's flow :
His words should warn us all—
Be kind and true to those who trust,
If to ourselves we would be just,
Lest such our fate befall !

MUSINGS AFTER A MAY-SHOWER.

The genial rain with sunshine mingled fell,
And balmy freshness breathes from hill and dell ;
Each leafy bough with beaded diamond gleams,
And to the grove attracts the glancing beams ;
That flash from sky to earth on wing so light,
Fleet fancy's eye can barely track their flight ;
Now gilding clouds—one leap, they're on the stream,
Or breaking o'er the plain, blooms winter dream ;
So glad and gay of earth alone might be,
Joy's youthful spirit from its earth set free,
These tender flowers, now gazing on the sky,
Drooped on their beds until the rain went by ;
Their blossoms shut, with thoughtful, loving care,
As parents guard their blossoms, maidens fair ;
But now, as if from parent's counsel given,
The grateful bells look up in prayer to heaven.

And who presumes to say they cannot feel,
That joy and sorrow o'er them cannot steal ?
Refrain ! Creation's ever wondrous book,
Hath meanings fathomless, howev'er we look !
Man's vaunted reason vainly strives to form,
A simple blade of grass, a mite, a worm ;
Conjecture blindly takes a leaden flight,
And soon is prostrate, helpless, lost in night.
The flowers perchance a gladness pure may know,
When skies are bright and gales refreshing blow ;
The matin song of birds to them be sweet,
And murmur of the streams around their feet ;
The dew that glistens o'er them gives a charm,
The herald gusts of storm excite alarm.
The trembling air may have a sense of life,
That smoothes in calm, and chafes in tempest strife,
Each sound that stirs its unseen plumage known,
From joy intense to sorrow's tearful tone.

   .   .   .   .

The wanderer as he tracks the barren moor,
Who sees the future dark and stormy lower,
May err but little, deeming spirits nigh,
Who with him mourn, and echo sigh for sigh.
The thunder rolls, the heavy rain comes down,
Swift, herd and flock, forsake the heather brown,
But he, unfed, unsheltered, on must roam,
And in the blast still hears, " no home, no home !"

MIDNIGHT.

The city, like God's-acre, showed no sign,
The vane upon the steeple was at rest,
The calm of sleep, like death no ripple had,
The mourner, toiler, slumbered unopprest ;
Perchance ambition fed the midnight-lamp
With some poor student's life, who yearned for fame ;
Perchance a broken heart throbb'd out its last,
The end of one, who vainly sought a name,
Of such the Angels may a record keep,
Such common things disturb no city's sleep.

The lowly shed, the mansions of the great,
Were undisturbed as lake when winds are still ;
The Monarch only in his gorgeous halls
Unsleeping, sleepless, nursed his stubborn will ;
His subjects, heedless of his Right Divine,
Refused the crushing of his iron heel,
Had dared to think, nay more, to think aloud,
As if the canaille had a right to feel !
No wonder passion scared dull sleep away,
And left Revenge and Fear to goad and sway.

" Down Constitution, Press, and people down ?
I'll have no traitor-pen, no babbling tongue,
The chain of silence settle on their soul,
Or other chains around them shall be flung.

What sounds are those beneath my palace walls
Like clashing timber—now the hammers ring,
A scaffold, and for me?   Vile slaves, begone ;
You cannot hang the Lord's anointed king !
They heed not, and their horrid hammers ply—
A monarch, like a peasant base, to die !"

Thus raging, fearing, unrepentent still,
Distraught, his room he paces to and fro ;
Believing men but as his slaves were made,
He knows no more, and nothing more will know ;
The ring of iron and the duller wood,
Still startling fall on his disturbed ear ;
He looks into the cold light of the moon,
Beholds a scaffold, hears his slayers near.
The night is clear and calm, no hammers ring,
'Tis but the stirring conscience of the King.

THE WOODLAND FAIRIES.

In the fragrant bells that untended grow,
On the woodland steep or vale below,
We hide from the glare of the noon-day sun,
And sweetly sleep till the day is done,
When evening with her mantle grey,
Receives the parting glance of day,

We flit unseen from hill to plain,
And summon our merry elfin train.
Where tender lovers lonely glide,
By woody lane, or silver tide,
We mock their sighs and tones so low,
And flitting shadows round them throw.
When mortal eyes are shut by sleep,
And Care hath ceased his watch to keep.
To some sweet Elfin-strain we trip,
And nectar from the blossom sip.
Lone Echo charmed doth soon impart,
Our sounds of joy to nature's heart,
And from her sylvan haunts, the strain
Is crooned to listening night again.
Thus hand in hand we gambol round,
And now we glide and now we bound ;
Pleased earth retains the charmed ring,
Fringed with the tresses bright of spring.

    But the breath of morn
    On the cool breeze borne,
And the far faint gleam of the rising sun,
    Warns us back to the bells
    On the hills and the dells,
Where we sweetly sleep till the day is done.

ENGLAND'S BRIDE.

In her beauty and youth, like the morn o'er the sea,
Comes the Daughter of Denmark to England the free ;
And sounds of rejoicing awake through the land,
For beauty and worth every bosom command :
The harp and the voice of the minstrels resound,
Through England's rich valleys and uplands around,
From the bleak hills of Wales, and from Erin's bright
    shore,
Come welcome and blessing from rich and from poor.
So come maid of Denmark, like morn o'er the sea,
To thy new island dwelling, Britannia the free !

No bosom so dark or so narrow we find,
One feather of discord to cast on the wind ;
What matter our clan, our opinion, or caste,
The proudest that puffs is but man at the last :
At least, for the time let all differences sleep,
Should they ne'er wake again, a full harvest we reap ;
Of peace and good will, what a world were it then,
To find such good feeling the rule among men.
So come Maid of Denmark, like morn o'er the sea,
To thy home and thy dwelling, Britannia the free !

The hills of *auld* Scotland re-echo our song,
Where the wild torrents leap, or the burn rins along ;
The shepherd rejoices alone on the moor,
Tho' the dark storm is looming, the herald winds roar :

From the Chieftain's proud walls, hark, the pipes' thril-
    ling tone,
In that Shieling so lowly, like welcome is shown ;
The heart of the Nation beats high with delight,
At this Bridal Auspicious, the promise so bright.
So come Maid of Denmark, like morn o'er the sea,
To thy home and thy dwelling, Britannia the free !

FATE AT THE HELM.

Oh ! let no tear-drop dim thine eye
    When stormy tempests blow ;
The Fate that guards our peaceful home
    Doth steer where'er I go ;
Till Fate hath piped all hands aloft,
    Small danger there can be ;
I'm safe amid the storm my girl,
    As when at home with thee.
        So let the wild wind pour its blast,
            And lash the roaring sea ;
        I'm safe amid the storm my girl,
            As when at home with thee.

It oft hath been my lot to brave
    The tempest in its might ;
But they who trust, are stronger armed
    Than warrior armed for fight ;

A sailor's courage mounts, as mount
  The strong waves from their bed,
He fearless braves the wildest storm,
  Tho' seas dash o'er his head.
    So let the wild wind pour its blast,
      And lash the roaring sea ;
    I'm safe amid the storm my girl,
      As when at home with thee.

'Tis true the deep may be my bed,
  The billows rock my breast,
But if with thee I may not be,
  What matter where I rest ?
If He above hath will'd my grave
  To be on holy ground ;
The ocean shall respect my form,
  And harmless roll around.
    So let the wild wind pour its blast,
      And lash the roaring sea,
    I'm safe amid the storm my girl,
      As when at home with thee.

THE LOCK OF HAIR.

And thou art culled from Beauty's noblest brow,
  Where locks of radiant darkness pendant shone ;
How strange it seems, tho' neither strange nor new ;
  That youth and beauty are so quickly gone ;

This tress with winter's frost is interlaced,
  A flag of care and sorrow, symbol clear,
Too few the years to cause this beauty-waste,
  It tells of grief profound, and sigh and tear.
And she, that was so lovely, joyous, kind,
  A living blossom, nipt by bitter frost,
The wit that in her charmed accents shined,
  In withered hopes, and early winter lost,
    'Tis pitiful, that such a morning bright,
    Should bring a darken'd day, a hopeless night.

Our paths have lain apart, and silent years
  Have left us strangers; error past regret;
Our spring-time meetings still my heart reveres,
  Their joy can never die, they charm me yet;
And if that face, where nature's lavish hand
  Had all her wealth of loveliness display'd,
Had lost its light, its rose, its high command,
  Affection here would brighten, never fade;
But why in waking dreams my sorrow wake,
  'Twere better let it sleep within its cell,
But ah! its slumbers heavy murmurs make,
  Within the heart, where it doth ever dwell.
    Dear silver lock, unto thy casket go,
    Poor heart be calm, accept and bear thy woe.

THE SHEPHERD AND HIS DOG.

The winter comes wi' blasts sae cauld,
   There's not a leaf to shield the tree ;
And now that I am grey and auld,
   There's nane to bless or shelter me.
I sit within the nook my lane,
   Each waefu' chair stands empty by ;
They mind me o' the kind hearts gane,
   And bring the big tears to my eye.

'Tis hard to lose a wife that's gude,
   She twines sae saftly round the heart ;
That trial sair hae I withstood,
   And seen our bonnie bairns depart :
The winter blast they feel nae mair,
   The storm may rage aboon their head,
No sorrow now ; no want, or care,
   Unkindness canna touch their bed.

Poor Rover glints at me as fain
   As if, poor dog, it knew my woe ;
His lightsome days, like mine are gane,
   His sight grows dim, his footstep slow.
My trusty frien', to lose thee now
   Would be the keenest pang on earth ;
Thou ever hast been kind and true,
   Nor once ungratefu' frae thy birth.

Ding dong I hear the Kirk bells gae,
    Ere lang they'll do the like for me;
They made blythe hearts my bridal day,
    They'll make nane sad the day I dee:
Weel, weel—why should a lane auld man,
    To ony youthfu' breasts gie pain;
They could na lengthen out my span,
    And I but gang to join my ain!

OUR GOOD MAN.

Our good man's blythe and hale, and never means to die,
But live as long's he can, who blames him? troth not I;
When we were bairnies all, thus bent and old seemed he,
Tho' now our bairnies bairns are playing round his knee.

Our kind good man delights to meet some friends of old,
You'd deem their youth returned to hear the stories told:
And oft he kindly spiers for some one long since dead,
He's heard on't oft before, yet wondering shakes his
    head.

His memory is not lost, in ravelled hanks 'tis thrown,
He talks of yesterday, that's fifty years agone:
And asks if winsome Jean be old enough to wed,
Tho' o'er that lassie fair some threescore years have sped.

His silver locks are scant, the very wig grows bald,
'Twas once a glossy brown, tho' now so grey and auld:
But auld things please him best, e'en stories often told;
His staff he would not change, for one of shining gold.

But would you win his heart, chaunt o'er some ancient
    strain,
Old songs and tunes I ween bring back old times again;
Then grief or joy by fits will dim, or light his eye,
Thus hymned by lays of old, good soul he'd wish to die.

THE MOSS-TROOPER.

Let my black steed be saddled,
  My axe keen and bright,
The clan quickly gather,
  We foray to-night.
The sun sets to screen us,
  The shrill piping gale,
Shall front us, nor tell
  Of our coming the tale.
We strike like the lightning
  Unlooked for and dread,
Our path like yon sun's
  Shall be fiery and red.
'Tis the moss-trooper's hour to stray
And sweep like the eagle for prey.

The flocks of our foes
Shall replenish our fold,
Their arms we shall gain
And their well-hoarded gold;
The noble young steeds
That the cravens have borne,
Shall us homeward bear
Ere the dawning of morn.
Now sleep ye or wake ye
Who e'er did us wrong,
Dark vengeance shall thunder
Above ye ere long,
The night shall seem day
With your homesteads ablaze,
And the angel of death
With the Moss-trooper strays.
Now clansmen arouse and away
And sweep like the eagle for prey.

How merry's the life
Which the bold trooper leads,
The laws of the feeble
He owns not nor heeds,
His axe and his bow
Are the wealth of a mine,
With them a true spirit
For nothing can tine.

Like the red deer that wild
O'er the dark moorland bounds,
With freedom he herds
Though exposed to the hounds ;
Uncurbed as the torrent
That gathers new force,
From the cliff's cloven brow
That it leaps in its course.
So mount clansmen mount and away
And sweep like the eagle for prey.

LOVE WAS NOT DEAD, BUT ONLY SLEEPING.

Believe not Love can ever die!
Tho' mute for years, and seeming dead,
A passing word, a look, a sigh,
May bring back every feeling shed.
The eye may coldly turn aside,
And yet there may be lonely weeping ;
The brow may frown in injured pride,
Yet Love's not dead, but only sleeping.

Love cast upon the angry blast,
Or on thy desert's friendless waste,
May vanish ere the whirlwind's past,
All traces by the storm effaced.

But after years, some quiet hour,
Amid a smile, a sigh, or weeping ;
He'll reassume his ancient power—
Love is not dead, but only sleeping.

record

THE BURNT LETTER.

At Rosa's casement beats the snow
   And loudly roars the winter blast,
And Rosa's tears in sadness flow,
   She weeps for happy moments past.
A letter ofttimes read before,
   She reads again with eager haste ;
It is the page, where one of yore,
   " I'm thine for ever," fondly traced.

" He comes no more !" she wildly said,
   And to the lamp the leaf applied ;
And o'er her frame a shudder spread,
   As o'er the page the flame she spied.
Love's record gone, her dearest care—
   'Tis done! regrets and tears are vain ;
See, on the ashes twinkling there,
   " I'm thine for ever," still is plain.

In crimson glow the words were seen,
  Tnen gently melted from her sight :
And winds that stole the chinks between,
  Dispersed the ashes o'er the night.
But sudden joy her heart oppress'd,
  That lingering line new hopes had spread
Tap at the door, 'twas him loved best,
  And " thine for ever," still he said.

THE WOODMAN.

The woodman with each sturdy stroke,
The echoes of the forest woke ;
His arm was strong, his axe was bright,
And swift as arrow in its flight ;
Nor ceased he till the stately tree,
Down tumbled, lowly as might be ;
No more to rear its lordly crest,
Its pride amid rank grasses prest,
The proudest of the earth must fall
There is an axe which levels all.

His labour done, the woodman mused,
And thus fate's stern decrees abused :
"Yes, day by day, my strength I waste,
But of its fruits I do not taste ;

The Squire this precious wood will sell,
Enrich'd, whilst I in poorteth dwell ;
'Twas Adam's fault, or I had now
Not have to live by sweat of brow.
Oh ! Adam weak to list to Eve,
And make all woodmen toil and grieve."

The Squire was passing through the wood,
And by the musing woodman stood,
Said he, "I've heard your heavy moan,
There seems a grievance, I must own ;
Come home with me, and you shall dine
On soup, fish, flesh, and fowl like mine ;
One cover only left alone,
And all the others are your own ;
But if that cover once you lift,
I cast you to your fate adrift."

The woodman danced in wild delight,
His fondest hopes were ne'er so bright ;
Thus like a Squire to laze and feast,
One cover matter'd not the least.
So to the Manor-hall he went,
Nor good-bye to his axe he sent ;
Arrived, he found a goodly board,
No Squire had table better stored ;
He laughed at the forbidden dish,
Towards it he'd not e'en a wish.

Day after day, the daintiest fare,
No labour, but there grew a care;
That hidden dish his mind opprest,
And gave much trouble to his breast;
" Beneath that cover what can be
That I must neither taste nor see;
It must be better far than all,
Just if 1 peep, no harm can fall;
No eye, nor tongue to say me nay"—
He lifts—a mouse darts swift away.

The mouse was gone, and he was caught,
To gain it back he stopp'd at naught;
Chairs, tables, glasses, all o'erthrown,
The mouse escaped, his folly known;
And in came flunkeys and the Squire—
Farewell to all he could desire,
Crest-fallen as the stricken tree,
And humbled as a man could be;
" Go, woodman, to thy toil again,
Of Adam never more complain."

BEVERLEY WOOD.

Within a wild luxuriant wood,
One bright blue summer day,
A woodman with his keen axe stood,
Like brute awaiting prey :

His large fierce eyes in anger roll'd,
  Now look'd towards the west,
As wolf might look into the fold,
  When hunger keen opprest.
His forehead low, his eyebrows coarse,
Lips thick, and limbs of fearful force.

Prostrate behind him lay an oak,
  His brawny arms had fell'd;
And now, the Minster bell awoke
  Fresh wrath, as deep it swell'd.
He muttered loud, his teeth he ground,
  And with the axe so keen,
He smote the trunks and branches round,
  Left space where they had been.
Rave on, he still his meal must wait;
Poor little Walter, why so late?

The boy had linger'd on the way,
  And let the food grow cold;
Now flowers, now butterflies had sway,
  He hurried not as told.
It is supposed he reach'd the spot,
  Where stood that hungry man,
But further history we have not—
  Each life hath but its span.
Thenceforth for him they vainly seek,
No more his mother kiss'd his cheek!

Long years have gone, few care to pass
　　At nightfall that lone wood ;
Where raged the woodman grows no grass,
　　Trees wither, nought is good ;
Winds shriek amid the blighted boughs,
　　Owls hoot the livelong night ;
No lover there will breathe his vows,
　　Each spring hath early blight.
The woodman lives, but see him not,
All memory gone, save one foul blot !

THE OLD MAID.

Oh, jest not Thomas, at yon quaint old maid,
'Gainst such, too oft, are satire's shafts arrayed ;
Thinkst thou 'tis food for mirth, that one should be,
Alone in this wide world, a stricken tree,
Amid the forest clad in kindred leaves ?
O'er such, sweet pity, outraged Nature grieves.

Perchance Affection, in the bud was chilled,
By some base trifler, in such vileness skilled ;
Deserted, pining, grief she must not tell,
Alone in silence doth her bosom swell ;
Ah ! who can measure out that poor heart's woe
That never more a hope or joy may know ?

Or may be, that her portion was but mean,
There's more of SELF in man than many ween ;
And oft he takes the picture for the frame,
And meets the world without a blush of shame ;
Upon his arm a rich, degraded prize,
While Innocence, alone, unheeded sighs.

No love, no sympathy, and friendship small,
What greater curse could human life befall ?
And, as her kindred drop like leaves away,
Time drags more weary, dreary, day by day ;
If such thy laughter move, pray let me hear,
What earthly woe might win from thee a tear.

THE TIME THAT'S COMING.

Yes, years sweep on, and if my span allow,
The silver locks will deck my wintry brow ;
The arm so firm become relax'd and weak,
And wrinkles mar the roundness of my cheek :
The voice, that now can give to song its tone,
Emit half-childish, broken sounds alone ;
The eyes grow dim, that pierce the vaulted sky,
And track the lark that up to heaven doth fly.
Ah, me ! This change must come, turn where we will,
The eye of Time and Nature follows still.

To be a man, the boy doth ever crave,
Would leap the distance, halfway meet his grave ;
But when his foot hath gain'd the topmost height,
He looks with wonder on Time's rapid flight ;
He clomb the hill, but cannot there remain,
The path lies downward, fleetly day doth wane ;
And as he views Life setting in the west,
A spirit whispers, " Early days were best."
Ah, me ! This change must come, turn where we will,
The eye of Time and Nature follows still.

At length, when darkening eye and shrivel'd cheek,
And palsied limb the journey's end bespeak ;
Some friend to cheer will gently blink the truth,
And vow my looks betray returning youth :
And I in age's, vanity may smile,
And half-believing, thus myself beguile ;
" Yes, truly friends, I'm hearty, blithe, and hale,
And not so old, that aught as yet should fail."
Ah, me ! This change must come, turn where we will,
The eye of Time and Nature tracks us still.

If to that stage, my lot shall heaven cast,
Friends will have fall'n like leaves in winter's blast ;
And memory failed to trace, upon the brain,
The once familiar forms ne'er met again ;

And those around will marvel much to hear,
I once was young, had loved, nay, more, was dear ;
At age so ripe, who would not wish to sleep,
Who would not cry, " Come, reaper, come and reap !"

SHE CAME, AND SHE WENT.

She came like a sunbeam that wakens the flowers,
Then leaves them as quickly to darkness and showers ;
Sly Cupid around her his bow ever plies,
But pangs there are none, 'till we lose her bright eyes :
Oh ! why did you come, rather why did you go,
Was such loveliness formed but for wonder and woe ?
Yet veil them in pity, those orbs, from all sight,
The world better lose, than expire by their light.

The tones of her voice are like angel-harps heard,
In·the calm of the night, by the heaven-dreaming bard ;
And her glances, that melt every bosom to love,
Are hallowed as saints, when uplifted above.
Her beauty leaves Fiction and Fancy behind,
And is only eclipsed by the charms of her mind ;
But she came, and she went, like a meteor so bright,
That dazzles, then leaves us to darkness and night.

" Thus a Bard swept the strings and his soul-music shed ,
In rapture, Hope listened, no promise had fled ;

Oh ! sweet days of poesy, sweet days of youth,
How enchanting your dreams to the cold chilling truth :
He knew not of falsehood, believed not in change,
Thus loving through life they together would range ;
Dreams quickly dispelled, soon their paths lay apart,
And a sorrow was cast, on his Harp and his Heart."

THE CAULD BLASTS O' WINTER.

Be sure dear wife your claithings gude,
The blasts enough to freeze the bluid ;
Wi' awfu' swirl it shakes the door,
And gars the chimney reek and roar :
Tho' aft beneath the cauld moonbeam,
We've roam'd by frozen bank and stream ;
Now thou art grey and I am bald,
E'en love will scarce keep out the cauld.

Time was when yonder murky sky,
And blinding snaw drifts whirling by ;
And swollen streams, and pathless moor,
A' couldna keep me frae your door :
Hey, lassie, were we noo apart,
Tho' love still lows within my heart ;
Should I on sicna errand fa',
I'd sure be smoor'd amang the snaw.

And ye that used to dance sae weel,
And bang the lave at jig or reel,
Could hardly cross the buckle noo,
For blythest lilt e'er piper blew :
But we have danced and we have sung,
Like ithers, have been blythe and young ;
Our bairns—nane better could ye find,
Troth, heaven to us is unco kind.

And tho' we totter down the hill,
Hae borne of storm and calm our fill ;
Still let us creep beneath the bield,
Life's winter, blessings still can yield :
I couldna linger here alane,
Wert thou my faithfu' partner gane ;
But whilst thou'rt weel, and to the fore,
' Gainst sorrow I shall bar the door.

LOST FOR YEARS.

Lost for years, lost for years,
Mourned in sighs, and mourned in tears ;
Never could thy faithful lover,
Of thy fate one trace discover.
Is thy joy and beauty o'er,
Shining on the earth no more ;

Art thou like a blossom shed,
Mingled with the silent dead?
Lost for years, lost for years,
Mourned in sighs, and mourned in tears!

Or has fate to thee been kind
Round thy path each blessing twined,
Mingling sunshine and the shower,
As sweet nature tends the flower?
No! the blast hath reached thy heart,
Keen misfortune's keenest dart;
Pleasure could not light the breast,
Torn from all that loved it best.
Lost for years, lost for years,
Mourned in sighs, and mourned in tears!

If by other ties thou'rt bound,
Lover, child of fortune found;
Wife and mother, joy be thine,
But ignorance and death be mine!
If 'tis so, still may I roam,
Search on and never find thy home;
Or meet thee once but eye to eye,
And blest beyond expression die!
Lost for years, lost for years,
Mourned in sighs, and mourned in tears.

THE TOWER AND THE IVY.

O, harm not a bough,
Of the ivy true,
Let it cling to the crumbling walls ;
From the wind and shower,
'Twill guard the tower,
'Till the stern old warrior falls ;
Staunch friends I ween,
They still have been,
For a hundred years and moe ;
Tho' the Barons of old,
In their tombs lie cold,
And the castle's pride hath Time laid low.
So harm not a bough,
Of the ivy true,
Let it cling to its ancient friend.

It hath seen the prime,
Of the olden time,
When the halls with gladness rang ;
And the hound and horn,
Awoke the morn,
Or the furious battle clang ;
And the sweet young bride,
In her beauty's pride,

Hath twined her garlands there ;
　　But time in his flight,
　　Hath slain her true Knight,
And mingled with dust the lady fair ;
　　So harm not a bough,
　　Of the ivy true,
Let it cling to its ancient friend.

　　In life's bleak round,
　　Who hath not found,
Some cherish'd hearts grow cold ;
　　When his purse grew light,
　　And his hopes less bright,
And Care at his hearth grew bold ?
　　But a friend to the last,
　　Stands the ivy fast,
To the tower so worn and grey ;
　　Tho' its strength be gone,
　　And the blast rolls on,
Through the roofless halls in their last decay,
　　So harm not a bough,
　　Of the ivy true,
Let it cling to its ancient friend.

———

SMILE NOT ON THE PAST.

Smile not on the past, Ellen,
Smile not on the past;
Approach it with a reverend tread,
As tho' 'twere ashes of the dead;
Mirth cannot smile a wrong to right,
Or give a healthy bloom to blight;
From me shall no reproach be cast,
But smile not, smile not on the past!

The gloom upon my brow Ellen,
The gloom of heart will last;
Believest thou that a mark for mirth,
Mockest thou the grief that owes thee birth?
All hearts are not for change like thine,
Now fire, now ice, such is not mine:
.   .   .   .
Reproach from me shall not be cast,
But smile not, smile not on the past!

Pity, I would spurn Ellen,
Needless, none thou hast;
Onward to the end I go,
Bearing still my load of woe,
None to sooth or calm my grief,
Hopeless, but that life is brief?
Spare me not, your arrows cast,
But smile not, smile not on the past!

THE TETHER'D ASS.

One pleasant morning in the spring,
When wildflowers blow, and wild-birds sing ;
I took my way 'mid country lanes,
Through gates, o'er stiles, and daisied plains :
When from her icy winter-sleep,
Glad Nature wakes, so calm and meek ;
The dewdrop gleaming on the grass,
Who can without a greeting pass.
Health on the balmy breeze is borne,
And beautiful is young spring-morn.

I mark'd the golden buttercup,
And heard the joyous lark spring up :
Went, with the winding woodland stream,
And mark'd its diamond-radiance gleam ;
As merry sunbeams o'er it play'd,
And twinkling fairy-circles made ;
And willows bent to kiss its wave
That still a loving murmur gave.
Tho' neither blossom, stream, or bird
My heart, the self-same spirit, stirr'd.

Howe'er our pride may hold command,
The whole was fashioned by one hand ;
The primrose, with its modest face,
Is kin, tho' of another race ;

The violet, with its soft blue eyes,
No maiden beautiful despise ;
If it might speak, 'twould say to thee,
" Thy father, sweet, created me."
Yes, be it man, or maid, or flower,
All—all obey the self-same power !

Amid a field of dewy grass
I found a stubborn, hungry ass ;
Fast tether'd to an ample stake,
Round which he might a circle make :
His dull perception fail'd to see,
No asses strength could set him free ;
So blindly rushed from side to side,
Nor for a thistle would abide.
The ass who would his tether strain,
Doth find his efforts worse than vain.

With Nature's law too weak to cope,
The ass accepts his length of rope ;
And then, he took his circle round,
And much of pleasant herbage found.
Be satisfied, poor ass, I said,
From all I've heard, and seen, and read,
The greatest man is tether'd too,
He has his limit just as you.
There is a line he cannot pass,
One circle, like the tether'd ass.

THE LOST SHADOW.

" The red beams of the setting sun,
    The murmur of the heaving sea ;
Two shadows o'er the yellow sands,
    Together lengthening peacefully."
When all the storms around me now,
    When hope, and fear, and life depart ;
That peaceful landscape, death will find
    Engraven on my lonely heart.

The ocean murmurs as of yore,
    The mellow sunset still is fair ;
The yellow sands again I trace,
    But only find one shadow there ?
No more her beaming eyes I meet,
    No more her silver voice 1 hear ;
That gave to sweetest language grace,
    And made this scene for ever dear.

He idly mourns, who mourns in vain,
    Her, to restore, all tears would fail ;
Still fancy, paint the happy past.
    And cease sad harp, thy fruitless wail.
" The red beams of the setting sun,
    Tho murmur of the heaving sea ;
Twe shadows o'er the yellow sands,
    Together lengthening peacefully ! "

THE OLD STAGE COACH.

The old stage coach hath had its day,
And hastens onward to decay ;
The rail, for strength and speed doth reign,
The poor old stage competes in vain :
When first I left my northern home
Amid the sunny south to roam,
I met it by the calm green lane
With hope most bright, yet mixed with pain ;
And mounted swift, amid the cry,
" God bless you John, good-bye, good-bye."

Through many changeful years my track,
Before the old stage bore me back ;
How pleased was I to view again
The forest, hill, and flowery plain :
The lanes familiar features wore,
Their look of gladness, as of yore ;
My friends were there, with friendly hand,
With well pleased look and voices bland,
But some were missing—low they lie,
Who blessed me as they said good-bye.

The old stage coach may still be seen
In country nook and roadside green :

The group without, the group within,
The guard with horn of merry din :
Some youth or maid with friends around,
And boxes piled upon the ground,
Awaits the clatter of the wheel
To mount and off, for woe or weal.
Thus met, I seem to hear the cry,
" God bless you John, good-bye, good-bye."

THE GREY FRIAR.

" This storm makes a terrible rout,"
    Said a Grey Friar seated alone ;
" How I pity the poor souls without,
    And bless this good luck of my own.
Thus seated so snug in my warm chimney nook,
Never dreaming of penance, of beads, or of book :
Of sack a good store, and a bright roaring fire,
What more could the heart of a mortal desire.

Meanwhile he replenish'd his bowl,
    But ere the first cup he could drain,
A voice from below seem'd to roll—
    " Thou hoary old sinner, refrain !
No more shall you bask in your warm chimney nook,
Never dreaming of penance, of beads, or of book ;
Of the good things of life you have had your full share
Now with me you must come—toper, sinner, prepare !"

The Friar roar'd out with affright—
  Less fitted to die than to live,
I vow, if you spare me to-night,
  To the poor all my bottles I'll give."
Creak, bang went the door, but no demon appear'd,
'Twas but old Father Tim, whom each toper rever'd ;
For laughter, he scarce could cry " Sinner, prepare !
Your sack is divine, and I come for my share."

" Father Tim, you're a blockhead I trow,
  And deserve well the scourge at your back ;
The poor get my bottles through you,
  But I'll first if you please drink the sack !
Thus seated so snug in my warm chimney nook,
Never dreaming of penance of beads or of book ;
Of sack a good store and a bright roaring fire,
What more could the heart of a mortal desire.

THUS GOES THE WORLD AROUND.

  " Oh, tell to me you ancient man,
    With wrinkled front and crown so bare,
      Oh, tell to me,
  In prose or rhyme, of ancient time,
  When thou wert gay and in thy prime,
      Be frank and free :

Has life been merriment or woe,
Does joy or sorrow deepest flow,
　　　Is love's truth profound ?
You've journey'd far along life's way,
And know how the world goes round."

" Young friend, if I could tell thee all
The sorrows known, the pleasures flown,
　　　'Twould grieve thy heart,
Ambition's spur, the promise high,
The strength of limb, and light of eye,
　　　Do all depart :
Death mows our friends like grass and hay,
The beauty prized doth pass away,
　　　And cares abound :
I've journey'd far along life's way,
And know how the world goes round.

" I saw thy sire, an infant bright,
When first his eyes beheld the light,
　　　In ancient time ;
I saw his manly figure straight,
With fortune, love, and hope elate,
　　　In manhood's prime :
And at his bridal blithe and gay,
I danc'd the winged night away,

Syne heard the dull sound,
Of the cold earth heap'd above his head,
And thus goes the world around.

" So ask no more, but calmly wait,
And leave the stern decrees of fate
    To tell the rest ;
But be ye sure to bar the door
On evil thought, time cannot cure
    A sullied breast :
An honest heart hath joy within,
Tho' fortune's smile it may not win,
    And this I've found,—
Vice bows e'en throned kings to dust,
And thus goes the world around."

THE CHEVIOT HILLS.

Wild Cheviot of the heathy breast,
Thine are the hills I love the best ;
Shrouding their grey heads in the sky,
Parting the strong winds as they fly.

Oh ! how I loved thy crags to climb
In boyhood's glad and reckless time,
And loud my shouts of uncurbed glee
Were mocked and mocked again by thee.

And how I loved to see the storm
Bend o'er thee its gigantic form,
With cloudy wing and eye of fire
Sweeping the thunder for a lyre.

How oft I paused in wending home
To mark the torrent white with foam,
Roaring along o'er hill and dale
Hurrying to tell the sea its tale.

The thunder cloud, the swollen flood,
The ocean voice of the valley wood,
The lonely tree that braved the blast
Tho' black and bare its arms were cast ;
The sullen scowl of the gathering night
Unto my soul were all delight ;
And oft when toying with the gale
I longed o'er earth and sky to sail,
To distant lands beyond the sea
On its free wing, myself as free.

" OUR SIDE YET."

There's a land beyond the Tyne,
With its hills and valleys fine,
That I dearly loved " lang syne,"
And can ne'er forget ;

In the west the Cheviots blue,
Rise snow-clad the summer through,
To the east, with changeful hue,
  The wild waves fret :
And turn where'er you will,
Tower or castle tops the hill,
And each valley hath its rill,
  Singing sweetly yet ;
And at harvest-home or fair,
Should kind fortune take you there,
With our lads and lasses rare,
  You'll sing " OUR SIDE YET."

I have wandered from my hame,
And have sought to win a name,
But the dearest sound of fame
  Came from " Our side yet ;"
I have crossed the stormy tide,
On the lonely desert sighed,
Every danger have defied,
  And for " Our side yet :"
When the battle poured its blast,
And the death-hail rattled past,
With the brave, I thought at last,
  My sun would set ;

A ball had laid me low,
Life flickered to and fro,
But I turned me to the foe,
    And cried " OUR SIDE YET."

Stretched upon the gory field,
Soon I thought my breath to yield,
Nor again the sword to wield,
    For my own dear land ;
Night stilled the battle's roar,
Death knocked at life's weak door ;
Help came, when hope was o'er,
    From a Border hand :
The storm has come and gane,
I've recrossed the stormy main,
Like sunshine after rain,
    Joy my heart hath lit ;
To my native hills I'm bound,
Where old friends will gather round,
To the old heart-stirring sound
    Of the " OUR SIDE YET."

FLIGHT OF THE MURDERER.

Slowly adown the Thames a vessel glides,
    And on the deck are some instinct with hope ;
With others, deep and dark regret abides,
And ardent souls, who 'gainst all odds would cope :

To those of bold adventure, change is life,
    A foreign land must furnish wealth and fame ;
But calmer natures fear both change and strife,
    Their home and kindred, all the heart doth claim.
Upon the deck, half hid, sits one alone,
    Whose heart to all but self, is as a stone.

His restless eyes towards London ever strain,
    And fretfully he marks each following sail ;
Each step approaching startles his wild brain,
    He curses inwardly the sleeping gale ;
Oh ! that the winds would wake and sweep him on,
    The hurricane, the thunder dark he'd hail ;
From England's dreaded shores he would begone,
    That seemeth heaven to him, let all else fail.
To fly from God or man's a hopeless flight,
    Or from ourselves, when sin hath cast a blight.

The vessel now scuds o'er the flashing sea,
    Fate seems to favour that mysterious man ;
And all have sought accustomed rest but he,
    The fading horizon he still doth scan :
The gale blows stronger, night hath sea and skies,
    The mariner doth warn him down below ;
And now *secure*, his mad excitement dies,
    And to his couch, he weak and faint doth go.
No thanks to God came from his tongue or heart,
    Success, escape, were of, and by his art.

The tempest raged unheeded, and that head
   Upon the pillow, seeming calm was laid ;
Reflection came, convinced him that the dead
   Can tell no tales ; how could he be afraid ?
He slept, but conscience o'er his troubled brain
   Drew pictures both of punishment and crime ;
And now he was a boy without a stain,
   And then a planter in a sunny clime ;
All ended, with a crowd, a scaffold, rope,
   A Calcraft, and a death devoid of hope !

THE FALLEN ROSE.

In yonder vale a Rose once grew,
   Of peerless beauty,
To praise its form and grace and hue,
   Seemed Angels' duty :
Its spring was fair, its spring was bright,
And nature nursed it with delight.

A heavy storm this joy o'erthrew,
   A ruffian blast,
Within its wings the blossom drew,
   And laughing passed ;
The stem remained a sullen blot,
The rose by all save me forgot.

Mournfully the night-breeze round it,
    Through its wind harp sighed,
Pearl'd with tears sweet morning found it,
    Flashed bright hope, and died :
The Rose no more will nature grace,
For ever locked in night's embrace.
In yonder vale, a maiden grew
    Of peerless beauty,
To praise her grace, her form, and hue,
    Seemed Angels' duty :
The Rose, 'tis she, of whom my lay,
But more I may not sing or say.

———————

THREE TAPS AT THE DOOR.

———

" The hour is late, go home and sleep,
    Thy brother's past a sister's care ;
It is His will, forbear to weep,
    Nor wring thy hands nor rend thy hair :
All consciousness, all sense is gone,
    In this world never to return ;
His frame for hours may struggle on,
    Be calm, go home, and cease to mourn :
Suspense is wrack ; when all is o'er,
    I'll tap thrice, gently at the door."

The sister takes her last farewell,
　　And sadly wending, seeks her home;
Each stone she treads on, could it tell,
　　Might say, " Yes, here, he loved to roam."
She prays and weeps, then to her bed,
　　But not to sleep, the years gone by
Flit, mournful greeting, round her head,
　　In each, his worth, she can descry;
Then listens, till each sense is bound,
　　And silence seems excess of sound.

A shock electric thrills her frame,
　　St. Paul tolls out the midnight hour;
She hears her brother call her name,
　　Would tend the summons, had she power;
No! 'twas but fancy; all is still,
　　But midnight is an hour of dread;
And now she burns, and now is chill,
　　Hopes burst to blossom, and are shed:
Each tiny sound upon the floor,
　　Sounds like three taps upon the door.

Each reveller that homeward rolls,
　　She hears his footstep from afar;
To her, it is the death-bell tolls,
　　Each footstep on her heart doth jar:

But one by one they pass away,
    And still no taps, to speak of death ;
And now, the sweet faint dawn of day
    So beautiful, gives hope new breath :
" All shall be well, I'll fear no more"—
    Hush ! one, two, three taps at her door !

RARE JOHN HOBBS.

John Hobbs is as sour as a man can be
    When it rains or blows and the corn's unripe ;
But see him at eve, he is brimful of glee,
    With his old brown jug, his friend, and pipe ;
For why, John Hobbs is a true Briton born,
    Complains at will that nothing is right ;
He rails at the times, all change doth scorn,
    Tho' rolling in plenty from morn to night.
                  Oh, rare John Hobbs !

John Hobbs inhabits a mansion grey,
    That chatters in storms like schoolboy cold ;
There raves the blast, like an organ at play,
    Through walls infirm, and through rafters old ;
Says John, " This house is my castle, I trow,
    The home of my fathers for ages gone by ;
They thought it was good, so I think it too—
    Our forefathers' wisdom let no man decry !"
                  Oh, rare John Hobbs !

John holds the proud man as a blot on the earth,
 And yet there is no wight prouder than John ;
He boasts of his country, his wealth, and his birth,
 Recounts the brave deeds of our heroes gone :
One moment his land is the land of the free,
 Then, rulers are tyrants, the people but slaves ;
For John, like his forefathers, will not agree,
 Believes in himself, and oft reason outbraves.
      Oh, rare John Hobbs !

The time's coming fast when John Hobbs must lie
 In the old churchyard where his fathers sleep ;
" No matter," says he, " for we all must die,
 Who best doth sow, the best shall reap !"
And still he is ready to aid the distress'd,
 As brethren, the children of sorrow reveres ;
Pale charity ne'er knock'd in vain at his breast,
 He gives with delight, and it shines through his tears.
      Oh, rare John Hobbs !

THE EMPTY CAGE.

Each morning dawn, fair Lucy sought
The happy bird within her cage,
And to him food and water brought,
And toyed him into mimic rage :

Then gushing from his tuneful throat
Came strains so clear, and full of glee,
A soul seem'd born in every note
That smiled and died in ecstacy,
The cage unbarr'd, around he'd stray,
But never dream'd to wing away.

One morn within a leafy nook
A thorn-entangled bird she found,
And pitying him, her flowers forsook,
And tenderly his wings unbound.
Ah! fickle maid, ah! fatal prize
She bore him home, and caged him too
And tended him with smiles and sighs,
Tho' he still strange and stranger grew,
Perchance for one afar he pined,
And longed to seek her on the wind.

Her early favourite now forgot
Pours forth his tender lays in vain;
She passes on and heeds him not
Till silence falls upon his strain.
'Twas love! not bars, that him confined;
Unkindness liberates the slave;
His wings soon quiver on the wind,
And not one parting note he gave!
Love from her cage has fled away,
And will no more to Lucy stray.

WOMAN'S FIRST LOVE.

When the spring-time of youth,
  Unbedimm'd by a care,
Gives to woman such charms
  As an angel might wear;
With the rose on her cheek
  And a bright sunny eye,
Like the fresh tints that blend
  In the young morning sky;
With a bosom as stainless
  As cloud-cradled snow,
With thoughts, that from Truth's
  Gushing fountain still flow;
Then her fond heart admits
  What its peace soon may sever,
First Love, and it lasts
  With dear woman for ever!

She loves, and her beauty
  Commands a return,
But love, thus commanded,
  May soon cease to burn;
And lovers, 'tis said,
  Often cease to pursue,
When their love is return'd,
  And poor woman must rue!

Now quickly deserted
  Fresh triflers appear,
To flatter and sigh,
  Many false, few sincere ;
But mourning in silence,
  She heeds them, oh ! never,
For she has loved once,
  And that once is for ever !

The language of love
  Coldly falls on her ear,
The lips breathe it not
  That alone made it dear ;
All tenderness still,
  Icy-hearted she's named,
Tho' eternal her love,
  As unloving she's blamed ;
Now perchance a sad change—
  When all hope has departed,
Her smiles come afresh
  Tho' she's half broken hearted ;
With many she flirts,
  And seems faithless, for never
Loves woman again,
  It is once and for ever.

WINTER AND CHARITY.

Winter bleak, and winter cold,
Spare the forms no blankets fold ;
Pause not in that narrow street,
Freeze not early lambs that bleat ;
Fly to haunts by fortune blest,
Vent thine anger on the west ;
Tempests hoarse may rave and shout,
Heard from blazing hearths without ;
But want and woe, and hunger meet,
Within that dismal, narrow street.

Mothers, with their babes new-born,
Huddled wretches most forlorn ;
New year chimes but mock their grief,
Hope is gone, still no relief.
Keen is winter's arrow there,
Shot through chinks and roof so bare ;
Shivering limb and hopeless heart,
Death ! how welcome were thy dart !
And want and woe, and hunger meet,
Within that dismal, narrow street.

Start not wealth, nor hide thy face,
Children those of Adam's race ;
Brother, sister, claims are loud,
Be not deaf nor fortune-proud :

Each who feeds on dainty fare,
  In such cause some pence could spare ;
  Pause not, for the timely dole,
  Scanty, yet may save a soul ;
And each can find the narrow street,
Where want and woe, and hunger meet.

  Want, prolific is of crime,
  Mother fruitful throughout time ;
  Labour's children guard from her,
  Then 'mong many, few will err.
  Winter, with its surly roar,
  Ope's to want poor labour's door ;
  Charity ! its step arrest,
  Give thy blessing, and be blest.
Fear not, you cannot miss the street,
Where want and woe, and hunger meet."

THE FADED ROSE.

I have a faded rose,
  That was given me long ago ;
The sweetest flower that blows,
  Could not charm my fancy so :

How changed it is by years,
 Nature would not know her own ;
And memory oft with tears,
 Recalls the beauty flown :
But why it moves me so,
Ah ! I would not have you know.

I saw it where it blew,
 In the garden long ago ;
In sunshine and in dew,
 Rock'd by zephyr to and fro :
I saw its beauteous head,
 On an angel-breast recline ;
'And ere the bloom was dead,
 The hallowed rose was mine :
But why it charms me so,
Ah ! I would not have you know.

The rainbow hues divine,
 Are born in weeping skies ;
So memory still doth shine
 Through bright but tearful eyes :
That scentless, blighted rose,
 O'er memory holds a spell ;
And mingled joys and woes,
 Around it ever swell :
But why it moves me so,
Ah ! I would not have you know.

OLD TIMES.

"Old Times" the fond heart still reveres,
Tho' they did mingle smiles and tears;
And oft, awoke by some old strain,
They come with hope and joy again.
O, surely there was bliss divine,
Shed o'er the path of " auld-lang-syne ;"
No friends like those of old we find,
No eyes so bright, no hearts so kind.

"Old Times," with you I thread again
The greenwood cool, the sunny plain ;
I see the careless herds at play,
And list the shepherd's roundelay :
Now wander by the sedgy rill,
Now echo wake from glen and hill ;
Now watch the swallow sweep and soar,
With all the early joy of yore.

"Old Times," dear times, with you I roam,
You lead me childlike to my home ;
There, seated in his oaken chair,
My father fondly smooths my hair :
My mother sews, my sister sings—
How sweet, how sad, her cadence rings—
No more ! fond memory close the scene,
I dare not dwell on what hath been.

" Old Times, old Times," oh, linger yet
  Nor joy nor grief, would I forget,
  But have them o'er the bosom stray
  Like sun and shade on breezy day ;
  And thus I'd journey to the last,
  Till with your light, my light hath past,
  And as my steps draw near the fold,
  Be lull'd to rest by lays of old.

A WALK IN THE WOODS.

I walk'd with Fanny in the wood,
  The farmhouse stood close by,
The morn was bright, the path was good,
  The breeze was but a sigh.
I had some thoughts I dared not speak,
  So spoke of aught beside ;
The charm of flow'rs, in language weak,
  The streamlet's rippling tide ;
The hum of bees, the falling leaf,
From which I drew a moral brief.

And oft, as if by chance, my eyes
  Glanced o'er her beauteous face,
But quickly turned away, the skies,
  The woods, I seem'd to trace.

Tho' nature's charms were spread around,
   They were as nought to me;
I worship'd her with love profound,
   But spoke of flower or tree.
Oh, what a coward was I then,
But love makes cowards of most men.

A sudden cloud the skies o'ercast,
   In sullen gusts, the wind
Above our heads went swelling past,
   The sun no longer shin'd.
The rain came pattering o'er the leaves
   And dimpling o'er the stream;
The radiant morn no more deceives,
   'Twas like a morning dream.
Beneath an oak's gigantic arms,
We shelter'd from the storm's alarms.

I had a mantle o'er my arm,
   That o'er her form I placed;
I knew 'twould shield her from all harm,
   'Twas ne'er before so graced.
But she refused its ample fold,
   Unless I shared a part;
It oft had fenc'd me from the cold,
   Now it reveal'd my heart.
Suffice it, I regain'd my tongue,
But what I said need not be sung.

A TALE OF YESTERDAY.

A fonder meeting could not be,
Their hearts were tuned to ecstasy,
Such bliss intense, on earth to gain,
Would well repay a life of pain:
Oh! happy youth, oh! happy maid,
How bright hath Love the world arrayed;
How like a dream, Life glides away,
But 'tis a tale of yesterday.

To part a pair so fond, so true,
No power of earth would dare to do;
'Twould melt a tyrant heart to tears,
And shed o'er youth the frost of years:
Yet think you such a heavenly flame,
Endured for years and burned the same?
Reflect,—but ask me not to say,—
'Tis but a tale of yesterday.

Perchance their eyes now turn aside,
Perchance she is another's bride;
But yet in life how could they sever,
Having vowed to love for ever?
Love in youth doth vow and sigh,
On the wind its records die;
Faith may be to falsehood prey,—
Ah! 'tis a tale of everyday.

THE MOURNER'S FRIEND.

Dry thy tears and weep no more,
   I shall waft thy griefs away ;
Waiting thee is peace in store,
    Care shall wrack nor night nor day :
     Dry thy tears, banish fears,
I am every mourner's friend,
Rich or poor their woes I end.

Love and Friendship, lights divine,
   End in darkness, as the day ;
Festal halls and ruby wine,
    Baleful lights that lure astray.
     Dry thy tears, banish fears,
Tho' all else thy bosom rend,
Thou in me wilt find a friend.

Thou stand'st upon the brink of Time,
   Before thee rolls Eternity ;
Instinct with thoughts and shapes sublime,
    Which thou unaided can'st not see :
     Dry thy tears, banish fears,
Thou in me shalt find a guide,
To that ever-flowing tide.

Dost thou fear the gulf between,
    Cling'st thou to thy cell of dust,
Ever be what thou hast been ?
      To thyself, ah ! how unjust :
        Ever tears, ever fears—
Would'st thou such existence bear,
When my touch would end all care ?

Worn by want, and woe, and toil,
    Ah ! how welcome, death-like sleep ;
Sense suspended, dead turmoil,
      Who would not that blessing reap ?
        Dry thy tears, banish fears,
Better still, my narrow bed,
When health, and youth, and friends are fled.

BY THE LIGHT OF THE MOON.

By the light of the moon will you meet me to-night,
When the blossoms are closed and the stars are alight ;
With no one to chide, and with no one to hear,
The hopes of my heart I would breathe to thine ear ?
If the blush on thy cheek prove the tinge of disdain,
I am silent, and never offend thee again ;
My heart, like a hermit alone in its cell,
Companionless, loveless, for ever shall dwell.

By the light of the moon
Will you meet me to-night,
When the blossoms are closed
And the stars are alight.

But I hope for a blush, with a smile by its side,
And a word, or a sign, that thou wilt be my bride;
Then no hermit my heart in a cavern to pine,
To thee my devotion for thou art divine.
Wherever thou art, it must holiness be,
Euch scene is perfection, embellished by thee;
Accept my fond heart, oh! Believe in my prayer,
By thee I am blest, or for ever despair.

By the light of the moon
Will you meet me to-night,
When the blossoms are closed
And the stars are alight.

THE LOWLIEST BOUGH.

An Elm, tall and wide, on a gentle slope stood,
Where the breeze loved to sing, and the winds were not
    rude;
There, sunbeams would toy, in the sweet summer time,
From the morn's rosy dawn to the soft evening chime:
The green leaves abundant were seldom seen still,
Lightly dancing to bird-songs, or breeze from the hill;

Happy family of leaves, thus by nature so blest,
So open, so shelter'd, such motion and rest.

Those green leaves so equal, when scann'd by a sage,
Who with patience and wisdom had read nature's page ;
Were found as divided as parties could be,
Tho' so happily placed, children of the same tree.
Those, floating on high, were in sunshine array'd,
And those down below, ever in the cold shade ;
The mid leaves now shining, and now without ray,
The highest smiled on by the sun through the day.

They danced to the breeze, and they danced to the sky,
With a wing of the zephyr they sported on high ;
The lowliest branches, they look'd on with scorn,
The mid ones endured, they were sunn'd by the morn.
The seasons still change, and the wild winter blast,
Hath brought them all down to the cold earth at last ;
No more exultation, all silent is pride,
Distinction there's none, now they lie side by side.

The sage calmly counsell'd, the group gather'd round,
" In this family of leaves, your own history is found ;
However your station by fate may be cast,
One day, all are levell'd, borne down by the blast.
And ye of high lineage, and ye of high fame,
Shun pride, for the humblest the same parents claim ;

The highest gains naught, and 'tis like he may rue
If he ever look'd down on the lowliest bough."

THE DREAM OF LOVE.

All wearied with his fruitless play,
   Youth sought the cool refreshing shade ;
He to the greenwood took his way,
   And o'er its bloomy borders stray'd.
A couch of roses there he found,
   So sweetly formed by Cupid's hand ;
He laid him down, and slumber bound
   His senses in embraces bland.

He slept, and dream'd, and feelings new
   Spread ecstasy through every vein,
For Beauty o'er his dreaming threw
   Her fascination and her chain ;
And hope and fear, and woe and bliss
   Alternate o'er his fancy swept ;
He wooed, he won, a crowning kiss
   Dissolved the spell, no more he slept !

He who awakes from dream of love,
   Doth find reality most drear ;
Youth woke, the blast roll'd on above,
   The woods around were stript and sear.

The bed of roses where he'd lain,
  No more a summer haunt adorns;
Its blossom will not bloom again,
  Youth finds it, but a bed of thorns!

LIGHT AND DARKNESS.

Thou'rt walking in the sunshine,
  Seem to gaze upon the light,
But never more shall sun or sky
  Unto these orbs be bright.
The song of birds is on the breeze,
  The meadows flush'd with bloom;
But thou canst neither hear nor see,
  Dark, silent as the tomb.

Thy wrinkled cheek bears passion's trace,
  As dried up rills leave tracks;
Alike, thy joy and anger gone,
  The last hope fervour lacks:
The blushing beauty, who to thee
  Seemed life, and was thy bride;
Her name, thou scarcely canst recall,
  Or tell when 'twas she died.

How strange it seems, that thou hast been
  A laughing, rosy boy ;
Thy father's anxious hope and care,
  Thy mother's tender joy :
That thou so feeble, blind, and deaf,
  With schoolboys gamboll'd wild ;
And clomb the mountain, skimm'd the plain,
  A reckless, fearless child.

Where are those youthful playmates now,
  Where is that mother dear ;
And where the friends of manhood's prime,
  That thou'rt untended here ?
Thou canst not tell, but like a stone
  Reared o'er the silent dead ;
Effaced by years, show times have been,
  Whose records all are fled.

And yet, as dying fires emit
  Bright flashes as they close ;
So memory may flash back the light
  Of youth, its joys and woes :
'Tis sunset now ; thy sun has set,
  Fate soon shall smooth thy bed ;
And few will miss that tottering step,
  Or weep that thou art dead.

Is this the end of mortal hope?
  Doth thus the warrior bend?
Forgotten by himself, can thus
  The proud man homeward wend?
Ah, yes! all earthly things, as grass,
  Must wither where they spring :
Fear not O Man to meet thy God,
  To dust forbear to cling !

HOME THOUGHTS.

It chanced upon a winter night,
  Within a pleasant, cosy room ;
A coal-fire blazing warm and bright,
  A meerschaum to be lit full soon :
A wight whose city cares were past,
  Sought quiet, in his easy chair ;
He heard the wild unpitying blast,
  No matter, 'twas " good night" to care.
The hoarse winds threaten as they pass,
Yet placidly he fills his glass.

On moorlands bleak where storms are free,
  He'd met them, when but yet a child ;
Knew cottage crush'd, uprooted tree,
  Mad torrents, brawling, hurrying wild ;

In nature's savage haunts thus known,
   Storms have in London few alarms;
Fine shelter, that same brick and stone,
   That throws about its countless arms.
Thus thought the wight, for he must think,
   No wight can merely smoke and drink.

Pale memory, misty-mantle clad,
   Soon led him back from man to boy;
To think is often to be sad,
   Woe, deeper channel wears than joy:
And oftentimes upon the way,
   He shut his eyes, now hurried on;
But like or dislike, as he may,
   Each foot-print he must look upon.
In vain each fretful puff of smoke,
To lay the ghost reflection woke.

He'd often sail'd against the wind,
   Had often let the tide go by;
He'd sometimes utter'd words unkind,
   And that regret can never die!
His stubborn will estrang'd a friend,
   Had stricken love with heedless dart;
That back recoiling in the end,
   For ever rankled in his heart.

With this same wight no more I'll roam,
Good friends, instead, we'll look at home.

THERE'S MUSIC IN THE WIND.

There's music in the wind,
　There's music in the waters;
But sweeter music in thy voice,
　Thou sweetest of earth's daughters:
The Morning and the Rose would fain
From off thy cheek the blushes gain;
The Ocean, Earth, and Starry Sky,
To match thy beauties vainly try.

Away with ocean's pearls,
　And diamonds brightly shining;
No light can match her beaming eyes,
　Sunbeam and gem combining.
Arrest the poet's charmed tongue,
Her worth can not be said or sung;
Nor yet the cunning limner find,
Lest too much gazing turn him blind.

There's music in the wind,
　There's music in the waters;
But sweeter music in thy voice,
　Thou sweetest of earth's daughters:

And thou art good as thou art fair,
And witty as thy charms are rare ;
I worship humbly at thy shrine,
No more, for thou art half divine.

NEVER LOOK DOWN.

'Tho' the future loom stormy and dark,
  And friends fly to shelter, away ;
'Tho' calumny make you its mark,
  Detraction your efforts betray ;
        Brave the world's frown,
        And never look down.

When you're thrown 'mid the vulgar and proud,
  And your poverty's scorned as a crime ;
When dulness exalted, laughs loud,
  And with it mean sycophants chime ;
        Smile they or frown,
        Never look down.

The hurricane passes away,
  Black night ever melts into morn ;
The lightning soon ceases to play,
  Detractors are given to scorn ;
        So brave the world's frown ;
        And never look down.

'Tis easier to stoop than to climb,
  'Tis easier to fall than to rise ;
Look up ! and look upward in time,
  'Tis never too soon to be wise :
      In vain the world's frown,
      So you never look down.

AWAKE MY LOVE.

Awake my love, the calm and pensive night
Is throned on high amid the stars so bright ;
Bright tho' they be, thine eyes would them outshine,
So in thy beauty come, oh ! maid divine.
The misty hill afar, the babbling stream,
The plumed pines, the broad lake's silver sheen,
Will all be joy and beauty when thou'rt by,
But wanting thee, all nature seems to sigh.

The nightingale love-lorn, from yonder tree
Unto the ear of night, 'plains tenderly ;
And watchful Echo, bears the notes away,
And to the rocky hills repeats the lay :
The forest faintly whispers to the wind,
The earth and sky are calm as thy sweet mind :
This scene sublime, appears great nature's throne,
Possessing every beauty but thine own.

Awake, my love, and hither as ye stray,
The blossoms fair will deem if morning's ray ;
And as they wake enjoy a sweet surprise,
To find the morn less brilliant than your eyes :
A heart awaits with so much love possess'd,
Be thou unkind, it never can have rest ;
Accept its love, of Fate, I ask but this,
And cannot deem the world hath brighter bliss.

THE BANSHEE.

" Larry Macfarlane, your childer are sleeping,
And sure the night long I've been watching and weeping ;
The wind o'er the moor, like the wild sea is roaring,
The rain in your face, as ye plod, man be pouring.
When laving this morning, you kissed off my tears,
You have no been so kind for these many long years—
There's a foot at my door, come in my own darlin',"
A voice faintly murmured—" Oh ! Larry Macfarlane ! "

The latch she undid, and the door she flung open,
But there was no Larry, of mortal, no token ;
She gazed on the darkness, she listened in vain,
No sound but the wind and the fast falling rain :
Was it fancy, a form through the dark storm was gliding,
Or was it a bale fire, some sorrow betiding?
In terror, she breathed forth a prayer for her darlin',
A voice replied wailing, " Poor Sally Macfarlane ! "

" Sure it was not the Banshee, my ears but desave,
That my Larry is dead, och ! I'll never belave ;
Come home now at once't, come home, my heart's
    breaking,
It's never you'd die, all that love you forsaking !"
The bright morning's dawn found a Sabbath of tears,
Its light on her heart cast the darkness of years,
For its young rays discovered the corse of her darlin',
Borne home o'er the moor to poor Sally Macfarlane.

I WAS NOT ALWAYS THUS ALONE.

I know a seat some elms below,
    Supplying shelter, rest, and shade ;
And near it waters gently flow,
    And summer-murmurs sweet, are made :
When seated there I oft recall,
    The times, the hopes, for ever flown,
And sigh, as on my heart they fall,
    " I was not always thus alone !"

Sometimes I mark at quiet eve
    Some youthful, bright, and loving pair,
The busier haunts of mankind leave,
    And seat them half unheeded there :

And as they whisper soft and low,
  Affection breathing in each tone,
The words seem from my heart so flow,
  " I was not always thus alone !"

The sun shines brightly as of yore,
  With living souls the City teems,
And Beauty hath the look she wore,
  From dark and fair alternate beams ;
Love casts around its silken chain,—
  New links cannot the lost atone ;
Nor Reason check the solemn strain,
  " I was not always thus alone !"

THE SILVER HAIR.

Amid her tresses raven-black,
One silver hair sad Beauty found ;
And to her eye there sprang a tear,
And from her heart a sigh profound :
The bloom of youth, she said, is gone,
And winter bleak is coming on.

Her mirror found, some comfort gave,
No wrinkle on her brow is seen ;
And smiles and dimples chase the thought,
She's lovely as she e'er has been.

" Ah, yet," says she, " the summer's gone,
    I know that winter's coming on.

" No more on fleeting charms I lean,
    Good-nature, truth, grow never old ;
To those affection still doth cling,
    When charms are wither'd, passion cold ;
No more regret for summer gone,
Love stays tho' winter's rolling on."

JEANNIE DOVE.

On the wild sea beach were two,
    One charming summer night ;
The wind, like lovers' vow,
    Breathed soft, and the moon shone bright ;
And one was Jeannie Dove,
    A blue-eyed beauty rare ;
Ah ! who could fail to love,
    That form and face so fair ?
Yet ocean, in its heavy flow,
Moan'd solemnly, as if in woe.

Two hearts to love's sweet music tuned,
    In youth, with hope and joy before ;
The darkest omen had impugned
    Elsewhere, as on that lonely shore :

Yet o'er the sunshine of their hearts,
　　Like flitting clouds or breezy sky ;
Some transient fear a shade imparts,
　　They have a dread, they know not why.
And ocean, in its heavy flow,
Moan'd solemnly, as if in woe.

The words they whisper'd could not give
　　The meaning half, without the sound ;
Such accents but in memory live,
　　Alone in loving hearts are found :
This was a parting, far away
　　The lover must his fortune seek ;
Come early spring, no more he'll stray,
　　Return to wed, tears, kisses speak.
Still ocean, in its heavy flow,
Moan'd solemnly, as if in woe.

To parted lovers slow is time,
　　The winter seem'd like many years ;
Love trusting, trusted, is sublime,
　　And hallowed were the parting tears :
The winter with its bitter blast,
　　Like ages, o'er those lovers sped ;
With spring he came, his fate o'ercast,
　　The lovely Jeannie Dove was dead.

And ocean, in its heavy flow,
Moan'd on, but heavier was his woe.

SPRING.

No more of frost, no more of snow,
The streams have cast their chains and flow ;
The soft winds genial, breathe like song
The tender leaves and flowers among.
'The happy birds no longer mute,
Make music sweet as lovers' lute ;
And love itself pours sweeter strains
'Mong blooming maids and loving swains.
A theme more joyous none can sing,
Than hail to thy sweet promise Spring.

To those who've journey'd many years,
Their joy may shine amid their tears ;
The bygone springs have left a trace,
Left blanks, that nothing can efface.
The bright eyes quench'd, the warm hearts cold,
The shepherd left without his fold ;
Departed, loving mate and young,
No wonder, if his lute's unstrung.
Yet, while that life is on the wing,
With joy he still doth hail the Spring.

It seems awakening youth to all,
Whatever storms their fate befall ;
For nature bursts her seeming tomb,
All life and sunshine, joy and bloom.
The skies like early brightness shine,
Earth's tendrils blossoming entwine ;
Birds chirp and trill on every tree,
What joyous, untaught minstrelsy.
What time has brought, what time may bring,
With joy we still must hail thee Spring.

Suppose like thee, we winter cast,
Leave freezing glances with the past ;
The biting word, the act unkind,
The passions, wild as winter wind :
Forgiving injury with grace,
Good-nature levelling every trace ;
And casting off pride's iron mask,
Forgiveness too of others ask.
If thou such genial feeling bring,
Oh, how we ought to bless thee Spring !

THE HEART'S STILL VOICE.

Wild wind, that like the solemn ocean swells
  Through yonder plumed pines, whence art thou bound ?
What spirit in thy troubled bosom wells,
  What is thy mission, where thy slumber found ?

The wild wind hurried on with hollow moan,
   Now sank in sorrow, now in anger raved ;
Despair and desolation in each tone,
   And would not grant the knowledge that I craved ;
But then, the heart's still voice gave soft reply,
" All things in nature run their course, and die."

A maiden passed, a blossom, beauteous, young,
   And graceful as the wind o'er waving corn ;
Her voice a spell, as if a syren sung,
   The charmed tones o'er moonlit billows borne ;
The forest heard, its tresses sway'd and bent,
   The singing birds were mute, so they might hear,
And sylvan echo, fond responses lent,
   On every bud, and bell, a loving tear :
Unto my thoughts returned the same reply,
From that still voice, " All things of earth must die."

I saw a sage, replete with mystic lore,
   Who knew the law of stars, and sun, and moon ;
Could tell when swelling tides would sweep the shore,
   When comets would return, a curse or boon ;
When seasons would be barren, or most rare,
   A lingering winter, or an early spring ;
When lambs would perish, or rich produce bear,
   Read in the setting sun what morn would bring :

I question'd him, scarce alter'd the reply,
" The wise, the foolish, rich, and poor, must die."

I turned to nature, asked of earth and air,
   The heaving ocean and the sun most bright ;
" Why should we thus of toil our penance bear,
   Plod through the day but to be crushed in night ?"
All nature seem'd at once to give reply ;
   Though youth and beauty, health and strength decay,
Alike, the mighty and the lowly die,
All animated dust return to clay :
The soul, that finds on earth no home of rest,
Alone returns to its Creator's breast."

WERT THOU A ROSE.

Young Ellen sat within a shade,
An arbour wreathed of roses made ;
And summer with a lavish hand,
Gave odour sweet and breezes bland :
A fresh-blown rose caught Ellen's eye,
Of perfect form, and purest dye,
" I would I were that rose," she sighed,
   Her lover heard and thus replied :

" Wert thou a rose, I could not bear,
　　To see thy beauty fade ;
My heart would break to see each leaf,
　　Drop silent in the shade.
'Twould be a pang to see the sun
　　Gain one kind look from thee ;
Or soft gale kiss thy softer cheek,
　　Or honey, rifling bee.

" Nor would I pluck thee from the stem,
　　To perish on my breast ;
But on thy blushing cheek I'd be,
　　A dew-drop there to rest :
And when thy tender leaves should close,
　　As night's chill shadows spread ;
I'd wakeful watch the live-long night,
　　Above thy drooping head.

" And when the radiant locks of morn
　　Gleamed o'er the eastern hill ;
And nature's matin song arose
　　From greenwood, plain and rill ;
Then, as thy lovely face should turn,
　　All grateful to the sky ;
Dissolved in beams I'd soar from earth,
　　Or lost in rapture die."

ANGEL, OR WOMAN!

I can but wonder, harp and tongue essay
In vain her fascination to portray ;
An angel now, but soon her wit and wile
Betray the woman, with a tinge of guile :
She throws her nets with artless grace around,
And hearts, like birds, are in the meshes bound.

And all so gentle, innocent, and bland,
Of harm she knows not, could not understand :
So sweet a temper, nought to wrath could wake,
But thwart her will, this seems a slight mistake ;
Keen anger flashes from her lovely eyes,
As lightnings flash from thunder-riven skies.

Oh ! when she smiles, what sunshine round her seems,
The summer morn not half so brightly beams ;
Love, peace, and beauty blended in one form,
But weigh your words, you may produce a storm :
When tabby, lately, caught her feather'd pet,
Her looks, her voice, oh ! dear, I can't forget !

" Peace, rhymer ; would you have your love so tame,
Nor wrong nor insult could her breast enflame ;
So stupid, she no harm can comprehend,
And calm, when cruel claws her linnet rend ?

If she you wed can only smile and sigh,
You'll wish her less angelic by and bye!"

HOMEWARD BOUND.

Faint gleaming, through the morning haze,
   The white cliffs of my native land
Appear unto my longing gaze,
   With magic of enchanter's wand.
Hail, happy shore, long years have pass'd,
   Since I to thee breathed sad adieu ;
But all my hopes are crowned at last,
   Triumphant I return to you.
Droop not ye winds, swift bear me home,
From all that's dear no more to roam.

When on the desert's cheerless waste,
   With dreary blinding sands around,
Fond memory oft hath fondly traced
   Each haunt recalled, each treasured sound.
And when by savage hordes assailed,
   And dead and dying round me lay,
My country's honour never failed
   To nerve me for the fatal fray.
Droop not ye winds, swift bear me home,
From all that's dear no more to roam.

Dear land, I hail thee from my heart,
My footsteps soon shall press thy shore,
And ere again from thee I part,
This throbbing breast shall throb no more.
E'en now I seem to breathe the air,
Within my happy native vale,
And greet my love, so kind and fair,
Whose truth and faith could never fail.
Fresh blows the breeze that bears me home,
From all that's dear no more to roam.

THE HARP FROM THE WALL.

Dear Harp, that in silence and darkness hath hung,
With many chords weakened, and many unstrung,
Once more I awake thee, if only to wail;
Should I strive to rejoice, harp and minstrel would fail:
I caress thee with reverence and love as of yore,
But the joy of thy music will sound never more;
A spirit that prompted thy numbers hath fled,
Like a beautiful blossom whose petals are shed.

Thy tones must be sad; rivers flow to the sea,
So Life to eternity hurrying must be;
That fact we accept, thus our own day will end,
Yet our tears ever flow for the loss of a friend:

To the lost it is naught, he is still as a stone,
The loss, and the grief, for survivors alone;
The wealth of the world cannot stem fate's decree,
So the loved ones must fall, drops of rain in the sea.

Cold Reason reproves every tear that we shed,
Our hearts we may break—that recalls not the dead;
Waves rise in the flood, and they glitter and gleam,
Then vanish as swiftly as scenes in a dream;
And monarch and serf rise and fall just the same,
Save that some lying stone for the great bears a name;
The monument best, that endures to the end,
Is the record of love in the heart of a friend.

Dear harp that I waken, the wail of the wind,
And the sough of the storm in thy music I find;
Perchance it is wrong thus thy silence to break,
And this melody, broken, half-hidden, to make;
Thy chords so uncertain, my griefs scarce disclose,
And the world little cares for my joys or my woes;
But thy faltering numbers to some heart may wend,
That vibrates with mine, for the loss of a friend.

THE THUNDER STORM.

One pleasant summer day,
　　I chanced to stray,
With one so very dear,
　　By river clear;

To ask her for my bride,
　　My tongue denied,
For had she answered no,
　　　Fate, what a blow ;
Still dear to me that summer day,
Tho' many years have passed away.

At length, within the west,
　　On mountain's breast,
The dark clouds gathered fast,
　　Winds shivered past ;
And heavy pattering rain
　　Leapt o'er the plain,
'Mid thunder loudly pealed,
　　Flashed storm revealed :
Still dear to me that changeful day,
'Tho many years have passed away.

Beneath an oak so hoar
　　My charge I bore,
And whispered to her ear
　　To calm her fear ;
The storm, the woods that bent,
　　Unheeded went,
We knew not till 'twas gone,
　　Skies brightly shone ;
Still dear to me that summer day,
'Tho many years have passed away.

ELIZA.

And art thou gone, sweet Infant! called
Ere life had well begun ;
Like tender bud torn from the stem
When opening to the sun.
O death ! were there no broken hearts,
No bosoms crushed with care,
That thou must quench the new-born light
And crop a bud so rare ?
When last I kissed thy pretty lips,
Sleep on thy blue-eyes lay,
I little deem'd that never more
They'd sun me with their ray.
In after years thy name shall still
Be hallowed with fond tears,
When in the silent city, I,
Am lost to hopes and fears.
For not alone thy father's sigh,
And mother's pensive brow,
Speak memory, thy playmates weep
And wonder where art thou.
So late I saw thy tender arms
Around them fondly twined,
And trusted that the coming years
No harsher thoughts would find ;

But thou art gone, a morning dream,
A sunbeam in a storm,
A drop of dew, a lily crushed,
Speak of thy fate and form.
Eliza, poor Eliza; grief
Knew not so young a heart,
All loved thee—thou lovedst all—perchance
'Twere well thus to depart.
Thy name, Eliza, was my gift,
Thine own the potent spell,
That shrines it in our sorrowing hearts
As thus we bid—Farewell.

OUR COTTAGE IN THE VALE.

I remember many forms
That were dear in early years,
When life was like the sweet spring-time,
Sunshiny in its tears;
From memory's pale, uncertain page,
The names have passed away,
The voices echo round me still,
The merry cries of play:
The old delighted who would come,
Among us girls and boys,
Grew young again, or seemed to do,
Amid our glee and noise;

And the Thrasher with his flail,
And the Milkmaid with her pail,
Are mingled in the memory
Of our cottage in the Vale.

When many years had passed and gone,
Again I sought that scene;
The leafy wood, the singing stream
Were there, our happy green;
And merry children blithe as we,
Were out with hoop and ball,
But ah! my mates like birds had flown,
None answered to my call:
Our humble cottage swept away,
The garden choked with weed;
Amid the wreck one rose I found,
A prize, none else may heed;
And the Thrasher with his flail,
And the Milkmaid with her pail,
Came mingled with the memory
Of our Cottage in the Vale.

BY THE RIVER.

By Humber's ample tide I strayed,
When night was dark, and winds were mute,,
The distant cities lamps were bright,
The city murmured l ke a lute;

The waters misty music made,
Most pleasant to the charmed ear,
I was not wandering then alone,
For by my side was one most dear.

The breaking waves in light most strange
Threw glistening pearls upon the shore,
That night had happiness most rare,
A light divine that shines no more ;
The Humber rolls as it was wont,
The city lamps yet brightly gleam,
The path unchanged o'er which we trod,
And yet the past seems but a dream.

Again I tread the river's shore,
When heavy night holds earth and sky,
And if no tear bedew my cheek,
The grief profound doth deeper lie.
The sullen flood with rise and fall,
Breaks on the shore with fretful tone,
The scene remains, the change but mine,
Hopes dead, hope fled, and all alone.

AWAY TARDY SUN.

Away tardy sun to thy home in the west,
    And bring the lone twilight so dear to my breast ;
For ere thou hast laved thy broad face in the sea,
    There'll be One by the valley-stream waiting for me.

So away tardy sun
　　To thy home in the west,
　And bring me the hour
　　And the smile I love best.

The nightingale's voice still is mute while you shine,
　But in the calm night wakes a music divine ;
Thus love in the bosom lies mute through the day,
　And pours out its soul by the moon's quiet ray ;
　　So away tardy sun
　　　To thy home in the west,
　　And bring me the hour
　　　And the smile I love best.

A shadow steals noiselessly over the earth,
　Lights twinkle like stars from the cottager's hearth ;
So love's light arises when storms gather round,
　'Mid the darkness of fate, its true brightness is found ;
　　So away tardy sun
　　　To thy home in the west,
　　And bring me the hour
　　　And the smile I love best.

THE SHADOW ON THE DIAL.

A silent shadow on the Dial lies,
　So slow its motion, that it seemeth still,
But from that solemn stillness doth arise,
　Dark thoughts that flow, and wait not on the will ;

While shrouded in reflection, time glides on,
 Unheeded, unrecorded in the mind ;
Look on the stealthy dial, all that's gone,
 By death's own finger register'd we find ;
Each ebbing moment to that monarch grim
 Belongs, and he is thrifty of his gains,
Will nought restore, nor trust is found in him,
 Life's goods and chattels, he at once distrains :
That seeming lifeless shadow has progressed,
Ten thousand souls have fled, or cursed or blest,

How many homes within that drop of time
 Are desolate, how many weeping eyes,
How many broken hearts in every clime,
 Life's sweetest buds, the dark despoiler's prize.
But time is blameless, in those moments brief
 Ten thousand souls most pure have flown to earth ;
The peasant lowly, and the lordly chief,
 Alike are filled with joy, and bless the birth ;
The shadow hath no bias, life or death,
 'Tis all the same, from morn to setting sun,
It truth reveals, or first, or parting breath,
 No interest wakes, its duty must be done ;
Thus joy and woe are ever hand in hand,
And ever everywhere, or sea, or land.

But what is Shadow, Dial, Time, and Death,
   And what is joy and hope, and what is woe,
And what is life, dependent on a breath,
   How shall we answer, that so little know ;
We may not weigh creation, compass cause,
   Effects, from day to day, alone we scan ;
They are His servants then, obey His laws,
   The uninalienable fate of man ;
And more to know, a heavy curse would be ;
   Who'd have the secret of his fatal hour ?
Who'd willingly each coming woe foresee,
   Who'd know each moment when his fate should
     lour !
Ere life's brief shadow from the Dial goes,
Up, watchman, guard each moment to the close.

INDEX.